"To the women of the world (better still, to the humans of the world,) THIS BOOK. Save yourselves needless suffering. *Bastianutti* and *Ford* target women but, insecurity knows no gender or geography. The myths they describe in this book plague us all. Hopefully we all will experience the freedom that results when these myths are busted and the truth is told."

–Sandy Krot, Director of Learning, Insight Principles, Inc.

"This book makes a bold claim: Regardless of how you feel, you are full of confidence right now. Confidence is what's there beneath the insecure thoughts that pass through the minds of all people. Through their raw and relatable personal stories, *Lana Bastianutti* and *Linda Ford* point us toward profound truths about our shared humanity that are more than just comforting—they are *eye-opening* and often *mind-blowing*. You will come away from this book viewing confidence—and maybe all of life—in a brand new light."

–Amy Johnson, Ph.D., author of The Little Book of Big Change:
The No-Willpower Approach to Breaking Any Habit

"If you want to finally understand where your insecurity is coming from; that nothing is ever 'done' to us even though it may seem that way; that we don't have to go through life believing we are victims of our insecurities, then READ this book. *Bastianutti* and *Ford's* deeply personal stories reveal that all of us are in fact, powerful participants in this life."

–Robin Charbit, CEO, Insight Principles, Inc.

"I *love* this book...with each chapter coming from a personal experience... makes the nature of our experience via these principles more relatable and accessible to the reader. I would recommend this book to *all women* regardless of their "station" in life."

–Cathy Casey, International Three Principles Trainer and Consultant

"Whether it be my teenage daughter, my college students, my mother - or me - this book can help each of us see the CONFIDENT SELF that lives within each of us. Read it once for the authors' engaging stories in which they share intimate details of their lives and extract lessons useful to ALL women, and a second time for the satisfaction that will come with knowing that you too, are a confident woman."

–Tracy Fitzsimmons, President, Shenandoah University

"Many women have told lies to themselves about confidence - and over the years these lies can begin to feel like truths. In this beautiful and thoughtful book, *Linda Ford* and *Lana Bastianutti* carefully and compassionately walk the reader through ways to transform lack of confidence into true, heartfelt confidence. *Bastianutti* and *Ford masterfully* light a path for all of us toward purpose, courage and success."

–Michele Woodward, Executive Coach, Michele Woodward Consulting, Inc.

"Imagine realizing that there is nothing to do to access your confidence and ease in life. Imagine discovering the Intelligence behind all life is within you and can guide you gracefully through life's ups and downs. Through their personal sharing, *Lana Bastianutti* and *Linda Ford* uncover the misunderstandings that many of us innocently carry around and take to heart. Imagine not taking your personal thinking, where these misunderstandings reside, so seriously and allowing your own deep knowing to surface and thrive. *Women and Confidence* explains a new understanding of the way humans operate that naturally relaxes our insecurities and lets our true nature shine forth. Read this book like you're listening to music, not studying to improve yourself, and you will find your life is lighter and has more clarity. Imagine that!"

–Coizie Bettinger, Artist, CoizieBettinger.com

"This book is a *gem*. It is the last book on confidence that you will ever have to read. *Lana Bastianutti* and *Linda Ford* do a beautiful job of pointing to the fact that when we come home to our deeper, truer self, we see that confidence and insecurity are both an illusion made up of thought."

–Sue Cross, Alzheimer's Life Coach and Legacy Consultant

WOMEN
AND
CONFIDENCE

THE TRUTH ABOUT THE LIES WE TELL OURSELVES

Lana Bastianutti & Linda Ford

This book is dedicated to all women who just want to be themselves.

Printed in the United States of America

Published 2019

ISBN: 9781793428790

Design by Will Mancini
wmancini.com

Contents

How to read this book

If you are already a seasoned reader of self-help books, then what you are about to read in this book may go against the grain, or may seem counter-intuitive of everything you have come to know about self-improvement.

In order to feel more confident, you'll more than likely be inclined to want to DO something and want to take some action steps to make that happen. That's understandable. We've all been taught that in order to feel a certain way we have to follow certain steps to create change.

Consider, however, that what we will be pointing you toward is NOT necessarily something to *do*, but rather something to *see* and *understand*. We'll be pointing you in a new direction that goes deeper and against all of the *doing* we're so accustomed to. Instead of alerting you to the symptoms of your insecurity, we invite you to see beneath your thoughts and below your psychology—to the *source* of your experience. It will be in the *seeing* that change will naturally occur and confidence will emerge.

In order to optimize the opportunity to see something new for yourself, we ask that you put everything you know and believe about change and transformation on the shelf, so to speak, as you read this book. For now, consider: *what if everything we are about to show you is true?*

Our minds have a habit of sticking with what they already know—in fact they like to judge and dismiss anything that may challenge what is already considered true. They don't want to shift gears. So, with that in mind, and to make the most out of this book, we ask that you pay more attention to the *feel* of our words rather than the words themselves. Much like when we listen to a piece of music, we *feel* the music rather than dissect each note. There is no need to engage the analytical mind.

We will also be writing from our own personal experiences and as such we have used the phrases: "I thought" and "I think"—and in doing so, it can seem as if we are intimating that there is something to 'do' with our thinking—that we have to change or manage our thinking. This is not our intention. The power resides in realizing and recognizing thought. Period.

We are going to point you in a new direction that invites you to see something for yourself. Read on, and we hope you'll see what we mean.

WOMEN AND CONFIDENCE

INTRODUCTION

Who among us has not felt a pinch of envy when we've seen someone who doesn't seem to have a trace of insecurity and exudes confidence? How we wish that we too could be as fearless, bold, articulate, and unabashedly expressive. How come there are some people who act as if they could conquer the world and who possess a determination to succeed no matter what? And then there are others who go through life as though they're wearing a coat of armor to protect them, and who believe they were short-changed when confidence was being handed out at the time of their birth.

And what is this elusive quality called *confidence*, anyway?

Everyone wants to shed their insecurity and feel confident. If that's not true, then why are there over sixty thousand books listed on Amazon.com discussing how to become more confident? That's a lot of people wanting to be confident. And it does raise the question: with such an emphasis on confidence (and assuming that people are actually reading these books), why are so many people still suffering from insecurity? Clearly, something is not working (at least not permanently).

Insecurity impacts all of us, no matter who we are or what we do in life. Usually, when we think of secure and confident people, we think of people in leadership roles: public speakers, entertainers—those who are in the public spotlight. But don't be fooled, insecurity impacts people in every station of life, even those of us who may appear on the surface to be secure.

In our personal relationships, many of us don't feel secure enough to say what's truly on our mind to our partner—we fear we'll upset them, lose them, or break their hearts if we speak our truth. At work, we hold back from giving an opinion at a meeting, worrying that others will find our ideas stupid or irrelevant. Or we put off asking for a raise or promotion,

1

believing that we're not worth it, so why bother.

And in our creative lives, books we long to write don't get written, and paintings never get finished let alone started, because they are too personal an expression for us to risk the slings and arrows of other people's judgments. And, in the bigger picture, many of us walk through life with little or no confidence that this Universe we interact with is indeed, friendly and trustworthy.

No wonder there are over sixty thousand books out there on confidence. People everywhere suffer from their own version of the belief, *I'm not good enough*. On a more superficial level, image consultants tell us that how we dress and present ourselves to the world has a powerful effect on how secure we feel. And for sure, success and confidence seem to have a certain look about them. Changing our clothes, shoes, hairstyle, and makeup can appear to do wonders for our self-image.

We're also told that body language plays a powerful role in how secure we feel. The way we look at people, make eye contact and shake hands; the way we sit in our chairs, whether we slouch or hold our bodies upright; it all seems to contribute to how others see us as either insecure or confident.

And if we're really serious about 'becoming' confident, we can even learn to train our brains to think confident thoughts. We can change our mindset—"fake it till we make it". We can rehearse and over-prepare an important speech. We can "feel the fear and do it anyway". "Act as if". And, according to new research coming out of Harvard University, a *Wonder Woman* pose can work wonders on our levels of confidence because it simultaneously raises our testosterone levels and lowers our cortisol—which is apparently the optimal biological mix for feeling and acting confidently.

All of these strategies can appear to work—but only up to a certain point.

These suggestions are all well-meaning, but the problem is that they are surface-level and temporary fixes, and they are all examples of our tendency to look for something outside of ourselves—something external—to make us feel a certain way—to fix what we perceive as broken. This is what we call an *outside-in* approach to our lack of confidence, and we will be referring to it many times throughout this book.

We wanted to write a book about *women and confidence* and its counterpart, insecurity, because we've personally met too many brilliant, highly competent, educated, and talented women who despite all of that, continue to second-guess themselves, hide-out in life, stand in the shadows, and play small in their work and personal lives. We too have been one of these women, and we find this situation tragic.

The intention of this book is to help you see insecurity—and how it shows up in your life—from a fresh, new perspective. In fact, we're going to turn the idea of insecurity on its head and boldly proclaim that it's all one big illusion that we've made up about ourselves.

When we understand that insecurity is something being experienced innocently within our own mind, from the *inside-out*—and that we may be inadvertently getting in our own way—that's when we'll experience the freedom to show up in the world unabashedly and unapologetically as our true selves. And when we're feeling at home with our natural confidence— when we have a certainty and belief in ourselves no matter what we've achieved (or not achieved) in life—that's a beautiful place to live. It's also the energy that will power our life.

Unlike most self-help books, we're not going to burden you with endless tools and mental exercises to change your mindset. We're not going to tell you to "fake it till you make it", and suggest you buy a new wardrobe or get a haircut. And you won't have to suffer the embarrassment of having to force yourself to do things you don't want to do in order to break out of your *comfort zone*. Although you may be naturally pulled to do some or all of these things once you connect with your natural confidence.

By all means, feel free to read books on how to improve your image, dress confidently, and how to look someone straight in the eye—they can all be useful and fun tactics. But there are some things that we just can't get from outside of ourselves. And you know what? There's no need. Qualities such as *confidence*, courage, creativity, and love—they all come from within, and there's an unending supply of them in all of us.

The good news is that ALL OF US (not just the lucky few) are already innately *confident*.

Right now, you may not believe that to be true. And you may be asking: *If I'm already innately confident, then why do I still feel insecure?*

Consider the possibility, as you read this book, that there is a part of you—a deeper self—that is already very much infused with ease, well-being, clarity, and security. We can refer to it as confidence, but it's really *home*—coming home to our deeper and truer self where nothing is lacking, and where we are whole.

Each chapter of this book will uncover a LIE that women tell themselves about why they are insecure. The stories we write about are based on our own personal experience. We have purposely used the word LIE because we believe that any excuse that holds us back from taking action, or that convinces us to believe that we're not good enough to be confident, or that insecurity is just part of who we are, is in fact a LIE. But we also have used the word LIE to get your attention. A more accurate word in place of LIE would be MISUNDERSTANDING.

The last thing we want is to have this book be yet another attempt to whip women into shape over insecurity; to force them to fix what they perceive is broken; to work at changing their personality. We're not going to prescribe steps to take, or have you engage in any action that is uncomfortable or embarrassing. And we certainly don't want women to feel any shame or guilt if they recognize themselves in any of these lies. We're going to explore this quality on a deeper level that goes beyond the intellect.

As the authors, our role is akin to being both a tour guide and an explorer with you. As a guide we point out something that may be interesting for you to see, and as an explorer we help you discover new truths and possibilities through reflection and personal stories. We can point it out to you, but we can't *make* you look closely, any more than we can make you have an insight (a realization) into your own understanding of your experience with insecurity.

Insecurity and confidence are actually just two sides of the same coin. When insecurity falls away—when the illusion experienced within the mind is revealed—our innate confidence shines through without any effort—without any tips and tools from well-intentioned self-help books. The fact that you're reading this book speaks to the fact that all of those well-meaning self-help books you read were never really able to go beyond the intellect, beyond our psychology and cause deep and lasting change. That search you (and all of us) are on illustrates just how much your well-being wants to come out.

The truth is: we are all confident. And every single one of us has everything we need to feel confident. In reality, we cannot NOT be confident.

Are you ready to explore the lies we tell ourselves? Are you ready to take the tour and see what's possible for you?

Be the kind of woman that, when your feet hit the floor each morning, the Devil says, "Oh crap, she's up."

–Unknown

I have a photo of myself as a toddler that I love. My eyes are staring straight into the camera as if to say, *"I know who I am and this is me, take it or leave it."*

It seems that for the first few years of my life, this is how I was—confident and comfortable in my own skin. Like most young children, I didn't have a lot of thinking about how I showed up in life—I just showed up and seized each moment.

When I reflect upon that child now, I realize that the personal sense of "me" that got developed over time had no real investment in how things in life ultimately appeared. It seemed that I flowed from one activity to another and one experience to another, whether marvelous or melancholy It didn't matter. Life was experienced with little to no resistance or attachment. Certainly, no consideration was given to whether I was good enough, smart enough, pretty enough, or frankly enough of anything. Life and 'I' were one and the same. No separation.

Somewhere along the way things began to change as a sense of 'identity' began to develop. Over time it no longer seemed as if Life and I were one and the same. Rather it seemed that I was separate from my experience and that I was separate from Life. I learned how to scrutinize, evaluate, and analyze—and to my surprise—I discovered that I was *expected* to care what other people think. Suddenly I cared what my family thought. I cared what my friends thought. I cared what my teachers thought. I cared what my neighbors thought. I even cared what strangers thought. Experiences that once flowed through me now became loaded with meaning—some I resisted and others I craved. It seemed that in seeing myself as separate, everything became much more personal and serious.

I increasingly found myself gripped by insecurity and uncertainty, and I became plagued by questions of *"was I good enough?"* I began comparing what I felt on the inside to what others appeared to be on the outside, and I learned how to please others in an effort to ward off their scrutiny and criticism of me.

As an adult, I cultivated a number of rules for myself that seemed to create the pretense of perfection and confidence. In my efforts to relieve my discomfort and insecurity, I innocently thought this illusion would insulate me from such pain. For example, I would go out of my way NOT to ask for help if I was struggling with something either personal or profession-al...doing so, in my mind, meant vulnerability and potential judgment and pain. It was all so much work, and I began to wonder and question my own efforts at transformation:

*How did I begin life so care**free** and **sure** only to find myself so care**ful** and **un**sure?*

And,

Why was my experience of confidence like a house of cards?...it didn't take much to tear it down.

It was in this frustrated state that I was determined to get to the bottom of what I thought was the slippery and elusive nature of confidence. I was no longer content to suffer in silence and helplessness.

I wanted to truly know:

Why was confidence experienced in some situations but not in others?

Could confidence be turned on and off like a switch? If so, where was my switch?

Was confidence a skill to be learned?

Why does it seem that some people ooze ease and confidence while I only pretended at it much of the time?

What was I not understanding about confidence?

All of these questions led me to pursue a degree in psychology and eventually extensive life coach training. This allowed me to continue my studies of the mind—I was sure that if I could just manage my mind and my emotions I could find my way to freedom from insecurity.

And it seemed to work. For a time. Sometimes. But only when I *saw* something deeply for myself. The problem was that my experience of confidence could never be sustained. Inevitably, something would happen and I would be flung right back down to feeling insecure, and the work of managing my mind would begin all over again.

Over time, I noticed that despite all of my '*efforting*,' that nagging feeling that I wasn't '*good enough*' was never relieved. It got to the point that I began to think that living life would require an ever-vigilant effort and that my relationship with insecurity was a battle I would fight every single day.

The thought of such a persistent battle was, in truth, depressing and overwhelming. It seemed to suggest that I was flawed in some way—it was as if something wasn't normal, or that something, some part of me had been damaged along the way.

Interestingly, I seemed to *know* deep down that there was something that I was not seeing. And so I kept looking, and along the way gathered more skills and techniques and tools, until one day I came across an understanding of the principles behind our experience of life. That's when it clicked. Somehow I just knew on a gut level, that this was pointing to a truth that when realized could change everything for me.

This new understanding wasn't about managing my mind to get me to a feeling of confidence. This was about understanding something fundamental in *how* the mind works. And not just for me but for everyone.

The key to freedom from my insecure thinking had been hiding in plain sight; it lay in understanding *how* our experience of life is expressed through our psychology. What resulted was a recognition of the mechanics of the mind that revealed the misunderstanding I had been innocently holding onto for most of my life.

It is my hope that in sharing this understanding, our own insights, and our personal stories, you too will find freedom.

I've had confidence in myself all along. It was just a matter of getting the pieces back in place.

–Dale Earnhardt Jr.

What if you were told at the end of your life that you actually could have stopped second-guessing yourself, let go of your insecurities, and discovered that feeling confident was effortless and second-nature to you?

I decided to co-write this book so that you and I don't have to reach the end of our lives and say to ourselves: *if only I could have broken free from my insecurities and done all of the things I wanted to do in my life.*

Too many of us hold ourselves back from expressing ourselves and taking action in both our personal and professional lives. I refer to this as: *Playing Small.* I have been one of those women. In fact, you could say I was "the poster child" for women who play small. I have spent a lifetime fearing criticism; hiding out in my work; not speaking out; not letting others hear my voice; sitting on my ideas rather than sharing them; over-analyzing myself with excruciating detail; being overly-concerned with people-pleasing; and settling for second-best in relationships—and all because of the pain and despair I experienced from feeling self-conscious and insecure.

My reference to *playing small* implies that *playing big* is preferred. Let me be clear about what I mean by *playing big. Playing big* is not (necessarily) about becoming the CEO of a company, or being rich and famous (although it could be for you). *Playing big* is about experiencing freedom—the freedom to express yourself; to not hold yourself back from doing what you dream about; to move through life taking the action you want to take with

11

a clear mind, and not to be put-off by doubt and fear. *Playing big* in life is when you know with great certainty who you really are despite the times you fail and fumble.

I like to compare this *state of being* to falling in love. Remember how it was when you fell in love (whether it was with another person, a place, a pet, or an experience)? You wanted to tell the world and shout it out from the mountain-top. And more importantly, you didn't give a damn what anyone else thought about you. You were in love. You knew it on a deep level, and that's all that mattered. That's a true expression of freedom. And that's actually who you really are when you come home to yourself.

I have spent decades steeped in the world of self-help and personal development, both as a practitioner and as a master coach. It has been my goal all along to help women live their best lives, and there is no doubt that the tools and techniques I have shared with them over the years have truly helped them deal with their insecurities so that they can go on to create the life they really want.

But, in all honesty, witnessing *deep* and *lasting* transformation in my clients (and in me) has been a rare occurrence. On the *outside*, it looked as if my clients were living a good life and making the occasional bold move, but on the *inside*, there was still a residue of insecurity, second-guessing, and anxiety that never seemed to go away. No matter how much coaching, reading, and support, or how many workshops—none of it added up to lasting confidence or lasting transformation.

There is no doubt that after a coaching session, clients would leave feeling inspired, lighter, and ready to unleash themselves. But they would come back a week or month later looking to *update their prescription*, so to speak. They still couldn't quite shake off the old and unwanted thinking that they were not quite ready enough, not quite professional enough, or not quite deserving enough to go after the great job or better relationship.

As a coach and seeker, I wondered: *Why are women still struggling with their insecurities, despite being coached, despite their endless reading of self-help books and participation in workshops? Why can't they experience the freedom to be themselves? Why can't we get to the bottom of this?* At best, my clients and I had acquired some really great coping and managing skills.

We've all heard the saying: "When the student is ready, the teacher will appear". That's precisely what happened to me. To admit that my coaching wasn't as impactful as I had hoped it would be was one thing, but it left me asking the bigger question: *Where do I go from here? How do we close the gap from where we are to where we want to be in life?* And the even bigger question: *Where is truth to be found?*

And it was because of my questioning that the "teacher" showed up with some compelling insights that convinced me to look in a new direction and discover a new understanding of how the mind works, how experience is created, and what causes true and lasting transformation.

I was also reminded that despite my years of feeling insecure, there were definitely times in my life when I didn't feel insecure; where my confidence soared; when I felt invincible; when I knew who I really was (if only for short-lived spurts). I wanted to know where those days went, and how I could get them back.

It has now been several years since I began to look in this new direction of the principles behind how the mind works—how humans actually create their reality. Why some of us flow through life, while others get stuck in the mud of life. And why some of us find ourselves riding dangerous rapids.

My journey is still on-going—there are days when I feel very much NOT confident. But what I love about this new understanding is that I can now see more fully how in the past, I would innocently use the power of thought against myself—to stop me from playing big. Knowing how the equipment of the mind works is changing everything for me because it's reconnecting me with the truth of who I *really am*.

I hope this book will allow you to fall in love with who you really are, because when you do, you'll be unstoppable—you'll be free. And that is the best news ever.

When you start to see the power of Thought and its relationship
to your way of observing life, you will better understand
yourself and the world in which you live.

–Sydney Banks

The Source of Inspiration for This Book:
The Principles Behind Our State of Mind

The source of inspiration for this book is the work of Sydney Banks, a world-renowned teacher who spoke about the operating principles behind how the human mind works, and how our day to day experience is created.

In the same way that the principle of gravity or electricity operates, these principles are operating whether we recognize them or not. They don't tell us what to do; they are not a *prescriptive* self-help tool; and neither are they a set of morals telling us how to live. They merely explain *how* experience is created, and *how* we can function at our very best in life given this under-standing.

The Principles Behind How Our Reality Is Created

1. The Mind Only Works One Way—from the *INSIDE OUT*: All of our experiences and feelings (100%) are created inside our own mind. Contrary to what we have come to believe, our experiences are NOT caused by external circumstances (outside-in). It is *thought* that creates our experience of reality. When we understand that the mind only works from the inside-out, we experience the freedom of knowing that no situation or person can ever make us feel anything. All of our experiences

15

and feelings are created and experienced from within.

2. The Mind is Designed To Thrive: it has the ability to self-correct. In the same way that the physical body has an immune system that protects us against invaders, the mind has a built-in self-correcting device to move us towards balance and well-being. This is good news, because it means we don't have to work so hard to manufacture our well-being. We innocently interfere with this self-correcting mechanism by trying to *think* our way out of problems. Less thinking on our part allows for fresh new thought, clarity, and wisdom to emerge and naturally take care of our needs.

3. We Are Already Whole and Complete: Everyone of us is already sitting in the middle of mental health and well-being. At our core, we are not defective or broken, and there is nothing to fix. When we stop reacting to our thinking, and when we recognize when we get caught up with our thoughts, our mind can become free and clear, and it is in this space that we align with our innate well-being that was there all along.

4. There is an intelligence and energy that lies behind all life—that makes life possible. We see this intelligence operating all around us in the natural world—it's why seeds turn into flowers; why a cut on our body automatically heals on its own; why the sun never fails to rise and set. Nature knows what to do all on its own. As humans, we are also being powered by this intelligence, our personal mind included.

What Do these Principles Have to Do with Insecurity and Confidence?

If the process of Thought is at the heart of every experience, then it would also include our relationship with our experience of insecurity and confidence. It is our hope that through our personal stories and insights, we will shine a light on the human condition and our tendency to innocently get caught up in the *outside-in* view of life, and how every experience we feel can change in a moment when we realize the design of the mind. Coming home to the truth of ourselves is always an inside job.

THE TRUTH

Before we begin our excavation into the LIES we tell ourselves about why we lack confidence, let's first begin our journey with the TRUTH.

TRUTH: We are all living in an ocean of thought. Personal thought. All day. Every day.

Because of this fact, we can sometimes lose sight of the reality behind thought. We begin to believe that we ARE our thoughts—that whatever is going on in our heads at any given moment is real and true. And it *is* real in the sense that *that* is the experience of life we are having in that moment. And it is in this experience that so much confusion and mistaken identity can be innocently created. We experience an insecure thought, and then we believe we ARE insecure.

Once upon a time, as young children, it used to be that we could be funny and serious; outgoing and shy; poised and clumsy. None of it was permanent. None of it was fixed. We moved in and out of whatever occurred to us in the moment. We didn't judge, personalize, or identify with any of it for any significant amount of time.

But then we grew up, and we innocently discounted any notions of limitation within our mind that we once held. We began to believe in something else. And before we knew it, we became what others said we were: quiet or loud; awkward or smart; determined or aloof; extroverted or introverted; driven or lazy; *insecure or confident*. We thought this was the truth.

The TRUTH is that despite all of our feelings of insecurity and not feeling good enough, we are actually all sitting in the middle of health. Our natural state of being is one of clarity, wholeness, contentment, and love. We are already full and complete of everything we've been looking for throughout our life.

17

While we may not always live and experience that place of well-being—while we may still find ourselves buying into the notion that our insecurity is who we really are—we invite you to consider that underneath and beyond all personal thinking, is a whole, complete, and perfect human being.

The TRUTH is where freedom lies.

The kind of beauty I want is the hard-to-get kind that comes from within – strength, courage, dignity.

–Ruby Dee

Reflection by Lana:

Women's beauty has been used as a measurement of their value throughout the ages. It has been bartered and dowered, judged and disparaged. It has been seen as a woman's power and weakness.

As much as we think we have moved beyond physical appearance as a gauge for a woman's value, we need only look at the media or our own life experience to see where it has overtly and subversively reared its head. Women are not immune to using the lure of beauty as a measuring tool. Consider how often we women unconsciously compare our appearance to that of other women upon entering a room.

We become habituated to this type of scrutiny from the time we are born. It is no wonder women seem consumed by how they look. It is an obsession that can suck the life out of…a life.

My own obsession with my physical appearance has played too big a role in my life. As a child, I had a slim build, and I hardly ever thought about my figure. I was too busy living life. During the summer of my eighth year, however, while vacationing with my family in Italy, I couldn't help but notice all of the curvaceous Italian women on the beach with their bare breasts bold as could be. I believed then that my bone structure and genetics would never be able to create such a body. And that's when it all began. At that tender age, I felt my first tinges of insecurity about my slender shape, wondering if I would ever look as desirable as those voluptuous Italian women.

As I moved into motherhood, and as my body began to experience weight-gain, I learned to camouflage what I believed to be my physical shortcomings, taking great care not to expose them to the world. Having two daughters of my own, I realized that I also wanted to shield them from feeling the same insecurities. I wanted them to feel free and accepting of their bodies, no matter what their shape or size. As a result, I was careful with my words and made sure not to express my own insecurities in front of them. I understood the effect that thoughts and feelings had on young minds. I just hadn't made the direct connection *between them* for myself.

My first real insight *into the connection* between how my thinking affected how I felt, came about when I took two trips in quick succession.

While attending a wedding in Argentina, I noticed that most Argentinian women were slim and beautiful—at least, that's how I thought about them! My all-too-familiar feeling of insecurity intensified as I found myself thinking a lot about my own appearance, weight gain, and lack of desirable curves—after having two kids.

Conversely, on my second trip, I went to Disney World and noticed that I felt much more secure and confident about my body and appearance. At first I thought that it must be because most of the women at Disney World were larger than the women in Argentina, including myself.

I began to notice that my *feelings* of insecurity seemed connected to my *circumstances* (Argentina and Disney World), because my *feelings* about my body changed from insecure to secure. I began to wonder if my feelings on the inside were directly affected by my circumstances on the *outside? Wasn't that the way it all worked?*

There was a hitch to my hypothesis, however:

When I was at Disney World, I didn't *always* feel confident. In fact, my feelings about my body and appearance fluctuated from moment to moment. In some instances, my insecurity returned with such a force that I resumed my habit of hiding my body or sitting out on activities that were too revealing of my body.

How could this be? How could my feelings fluctuate if my circumstances remained the same?

I began to wonder if the relationship between my circumstances and my feelings was one of *correlation* rather than *causation*. I also began to wonder what I was *still* not seeing.

The unfortunate downside of living with an insecure body image is that it stops many of us from living out our lives fully. We hold ourselves back because we fear to let the world truly see us *exactly* as we are. And we spend an inordinate amount of time trying to find ways to cope with our perceived imperfections. It is also rather embarrassing to admit upon reflection how self-obsessed and single-focused we can become.

My experience of feeling bad about my body only increased when later on, I developed a thyroid issue. That's when my confidence seemed to take a nosedive, as I gained even more weight. No matter what I did to lose the weight or camouflage it, nothing seemed to help. I slowly withdrew from life and limited my exposure to the outside world. And like many women, I turned to food to distract me from my uncomfortable feelings. I made excuses. I got busy with the lives of my children so that I could ignore (or so I thought) my own internal life. I would deal with this weight thing later.

I promised myself that, once I lost the weight, I could re-engage with the outside world and pursue my dreams without feelings of shame. In the back of my mind, I *knew* that my battle was not one of weight or appearance but rather one of discomfort with my experience in the moment, but I still held onto the illusion that my feelings were directly linked to my circumstances and to the numbers on the scale.

When I became a life coach, I delved deeper into the idea that my feelings and how I thought about my body were actually creating my experience. I learned how to manage my mind by creating better thoughts, feelings, and affirmations. I learned about Cognitive Behavior Therapy, how to process my feelings, mindfulness, and many more wonderful, well-intentioned strategies. I was all in. I was ready to loosen the vice-like grip this issue of body image had on my life.

Rather than finding freedom from my insecurity, this 'mind' work unwittingly made me feel worse because it focused the spotlight even more on my body. I felt an added burden to *think* my way out of my insecure feelings. My weight gain was now constantly on my mind. I also noticed that even though some of the strategies allowed me to feel better *some of the time*, there were also times when they didn't work. When this happened, my old, insecure thought patterns returned with a vengeance.

It was not until I came to understand the true source of my experience—how the mind really works—that I realized there was actually nothing to do (mentally) to manage my mind. Rather than *do* something, I simply needed to *realize* something. It no longer made sense to focus on the *content* and the *why* of my thinking (since that only led to endless self-critical exploration and analysis). What I realized was that if I wanted to feel true freedom from being bothered by my negative body image, it would require a shift in focus from the *what* and *why* toward the *how*— how the equipment of the mind was working to create my experience.

It wasn't *what* I thought that was critical to see, but rather understanding *that* I thought. Period.

My freedom lay in *realizing* that my experience of life—whether it showed up as secure or insecure—was being experienced through *thought in the moment*, and that the nature of thought is not static; thought is designed to *move through us* continually. My misunderstanding, however, resulted in endless futile attempts to prevent, limit, and redirect any *undesirable* thoughts.

The design of the mind is actually quite brilliant and hopeful as it continually provides new and fresh thinking and experiences of life. My freedom came from understanding that the system was designed to self-clear, and that it would always give me access to fresh thinking and a return to well-being and confidence.

By understanding how the system worked (naturally), it no longer made sense to insert myself (or rather my ego) into matters that were beyond my control. Why would I purposely *think* my way to feeling confident when doing so merely added more thinking to an already laden mind and moved me further away from my natural state of well-being and confidence?

Thoughts and feelings are not telling me about my true worth—they merely show up and create an experience in the moment. And just as quickly, they leave and are replaced by new thoughts and feelings that create a new experience. To believe otherwise is a trick of the mind, an illusion that is misunderstood as truth.

It is, perhaps, understandable that we innocently attach personal meaning to thought—after all, ego is a master of personalizing thought by linking it with the details of our lives and the sound of our voice. But don't be fooled. Thought is impersonal. It is passing through. Furthermore, labelling thought as *good* or *bad* depending on how we feel is akin to labelling gravity as *good* or *bad* depending on the perkiness of our breasts. Like gravity, thought is inherently impersonal.

I still desire to have a slimmer body. That thought is still one I hold on to; that is still my preference because that's what I want for myself. And for sure, I can still get tripped up when I experience insecure thinking about my body. When that happens, I temporarily become convinced that what I am experiencing is real. That is, until I remember how things really work, and I am once again bounced out of that experience as new thoughts create new experience.

When I understand how the equipment works, that thoughts (whether they are desired or not) leave of their own accord, I understand that there is nothing to do or add, but rather something that falls away. Knowing that our design is always moving us toward well-being, has helped me trust the process and not worry, or take myself too seriously. It's just how the system works.

Life is too short and too amazing for us to stay hidden or not engage in life because we think our bodies are undesirable or don't line up with what society dictates. Insecure thoughts may *seem* real in the moment, but there is beauty in everything when we look with clear eyes and an open heart—when we shift out of our egos and connect with the living, breathing world around us.

What This Lie Has Cost Me: There have been too many times in my life when I simply wasn't present in the moment because I was overly concerned by how I looked or appeared to others. I not only set unrealistic rules and expectations for myself based on my appearance, but I also stopped myself from engaging in things I would have loved, simply because of feeling insecure.

What The Truth Tells Me: I am not my thoughts. I am not my feelings. I am not my body. When I trust the design, suddenly everything clears and I can see how unimportant physical appearance truly is to living. Life is simple. Show up and serve. Play and be present to life.

Don't be ridiculous—a real woman is never too old.

–Cher

Reflection by Linda:

Seven years ago, at the age of fifty-seven, I agreed to appear in a video to provide a testimonial for a coach friend and her work with clients. When the final version of the video was released, I found it difficult to watch. I had never seen myself on video, and I found myself consumed with negative and denigrating thoughts about myself:

Was this how I really looked?

Did I really look that old?

Did I look that overweight in real life?

The sad thing is that even though I could see that my video testimonial was clear and articulate, even though I came across as confident, and even though my friend said I was a natural in front of the camera, I was still unable to feel good about my performance. None of that was enough for me. None of that mattered.

What mattered was that I hated how I looked. And it was that experience that would keep me hiding out in my own work as a coach. Over the years I made a few frustrating attempts to make my own videos and go public, but all they did was send me down a rabbit-hole of self-criticism about how my body looked. I felt shame, because I believed my body was no longer attractive. I was more consumed with my appearance and everything that was wrong with it than I was concerned about my message. Not exactly what you'd expect from a life coach.

Just in case you may accuse me of being superficial, you should know that I've spent an entire life benefitting from my looks—and by that I mean I have always been used to people noticing me, complimenting me, and being attracted to me because of how I looked. Indeed, some of my friends used to call me a guy magnet! And unlike most people, I used to love having my photo taken. And so when all of that began to change for me—when the face and body in the mirror no longer looked the same; when I began to feel invisible especially to men; the loss and grief I experienced was akin to losing a close friend.

I find it embarrassing and sad to write about how my preoccupation with my appearance—my awareness and resistance of looking older—has stopped me from confidently putting my work out into the world. After all, I'm a coach who talks and writes about personal empowerment.

But my experience is not unusual. In fact, it demonstrates how chronic this problem is for women. And wouldn't you know—seven years later, I may now have a deeper awareness about this issue and be able to write about it honestly, but I'm still not completely over it.

Here are some statistics that may shock you: Stanford Law Professor Deborah L. Rhode found that over half of young women today reported that they would prefer to be hit by a truck than be fat. Two-thirds would prefer to be mean or stupid. No matter how smart, savvy, articulate and enlightened women are, many of us are deeply, deeply affected by our thoughts about our appearance. Throughout my sixty-four years, I honestly can't remember a time when I was not thinking of how to improve or fix my body or my face.

We all know why we are this way. From an early age, girls internalize messages from parents, teachers, the media, and men. I remember my father (innocently) telling me growing up, how beautiful I was. Praise was never about how smart or brave I was. As long as I was beautiful, all was right in the world.

So we know where it comes from, but the question is: How can we stop it bothering us so much? How can we end our critical, daily relationship with the mirror? And, more importantly, how can we stop our preoccupation with our physical attributes from undermining our confidence to show up in the world?

Throughout my self-help journey, there have been two big TRUTHS I've learned that may offer some perspective on this issue.

The first big Truth: External circumstances have absolutely no power to make us feel a certain way.

We may be physically beautiful or believe that we're not: our bodies may be slender or overweight; we may live in a big house or a shack; have a great marriage or live alone; and we may have plenty of money in the bank or be living in poverty; but none of those circumstances guarantees that we will feel a certain way. None of it is the reason we feel happy, sad, beautiful, ugly, insecure or confident.

Are you buying this argument?

Many of us believe that how we feel on a daily basis is determined by the conditions outside of us. We think that if we can be thinner or look younger; if we can be free of wrinkles, maybe then out insecurity will disappear, and we'll finally feel happy and confident. This is an example of *outside-in* thinking. If we didn't believe this, we wouldn't spend our lives working hard, getting ourselves into debt, striving for material things, and spending billions nationwide trying to improve our physical appearance.

Outside-in thinking is the biggest lie we embrace and live by, and yet, let's face it, we all buy into it.

How can I be sure it's a lie? Because if every gorgeous, thin, and wrinkle-free woman was happy and confident, then maybe one could argue that *outside-in* thinking could make us free of our insecurity. But that is definitely not the case. We all know aesthetically beautiful women who struggle with insecurity about their appearance. We've also all had the experience of feeling great when we get a new haircut or wear a new outfit. But have you also noticed that visits to the salon and wearing new clothes don't necessarily guarantee we'll feel great? I can wear an outfit one day and feel wonderful, and I can put that same outfit on another day and wonder why I ever bought it in the first place.

I'm not saying that the efforts we make to improve our bodies and appearance don't make us feel good—clearly they "seem" to do this. It's just that those isolated feelings of confidence are short-lived and not sustainable because they are never directly affected by outside influences. Our experience of ourselves changes and fluctuates depending on the thoughts and feelings we are experiencing within our minds in the moment.

We're never ever feeling our circumstances, even though it may seem like we are. Rather, we experience our circumstances through the filter of thought. We're actually feeling our thinking in that moment. It explains why we don't always feel the same way under the same conditions.

The feeling of joy and well-being that we all want to feel is an *inside job*. No amount of beauty, power, or wealth can affect or determine our access to these feelings. They are already naturally within us. They are our default setting.

Convincing people that our sense of well-being and happiness has nothing to do with our circumstances—and in this case, our physical appearance—is a tough road to hoe. It sounds as unconvincing as it must have been when people were first told that the earth was round and not flat. It required a deep paradigm shift to see the earth in a new and radical way. But understanding that the earth *was* round did eventually happen. And in the same way that we learned the truth about the earth, we are also able to discover new truths about how the mind works which have far-reaching implications.

Knowing that the earth is round fundamentally changed how people navigated their travels since there was no longer a fear of falling off the edge. The same is true when we understand that our experience of life is created from the inside out. Suddenly, we realize that we don't have to control and manipulate our outside world. Life becomes so much simpler and easier to navigate.

Our *outside-in* conditioning is pervasive and deeply entrenched, however. And it is in this world of form—or the world of matter—that there's a lot we get to taste, see, smell, and touch. It is all so very compelling.

From an early age, we are trained to look outside ourselves to find relief, pleasure, and peace of mind. As a young child, for example, I quickly learned to take refuge in my doll, and I knew that as long as I could hug my doll when I went to bed at night, I would feel safe and calm. And sure enough, there were many nights when the presence of that doll lulled me to sleep.

Due to an amazing trick of the mind, I believed that my doll was responsible for how I felt. Children learn this early in life; whether it's a doll, a teddy bear, a pacifier, or a security blanket, our dependence upon these outside objects is just the beginning of how we learn to buy into an *outside-in* perspective.

We've all been heavily indoctrinated to see life from the outside-in. And it's no big thing if we fall back into *outside-in* thinking. We're not ever going to fully switch our *outside-in* thinking to *inside-out*. Even with this understanding, there are going to be times when we will get hoodwinked by *outside-in* thinking. Having said that, it still doesn't change the fact that the mind only works from the *inside-out*. This is a fact, whether we realize it or not.

As a young woman, my need for my doll got replaced by other objects or beliefs; and the big one for me was my belief that I had to be attractive and thin if I wanted to feel happy, secure, and loved. This became my new security blanket. And even though my physical attractiveness enabled me to get noticed by men, it still never guaranteed happiness or confidence. Ironically, my young, thin, and wrinkle-free self was capable of feeling desperately insecure and unhappy.

Women especially have been conned into believing that physical attractiveness will fix everything, but the irony is that for many women, the relationship they have with their bodies can be the biggest obstacle that holds them back from putting themselves out into the world, especially in regards to their work. And the saddest thing about this is that we women are investing in something that's illusory and fleeting.

How many of us hold ourselves back and hide out from speaking up, going public on social media, and allowing ourselves to be seen, and all because we're overly self-conscious about our gray hair, our excess weight, crow's feet, or the endless struggle to find clothes to fit our bodies? These are all examples of the lies we tell ourselves and get caught up in.

The second BIG Truth I learned: We are not our bodies—

When I was twenty years old, I was fortunate enough to travel to India, and it was there that I witnessed a public cremation on the steps leading down to the River Ganges. I had never seen a dead body carried through the streets, not to mention watching it being placed on a funeral pyre to be burned. To the locals this was a common and natural event, and they couldn't understand why I was so shocked. I have always remembered my Indian hosts asking me: *Don't you know that the body is just a vehicle for the soul? Don't you know that the real you cannot be burned or killed? We are not our physical bodies.*

That understanding of the physical body has always stayed with me, and it's something I've come to take refuge in. There have been times when I can look in the mirror and not recognize who is staring back at me, but despite the physical changes, I have never lost sight of the fact that the real

ME is always present and has been traveling with me my whole life. There are some aspects of me that have always remained the same, remained constant. We are not a beautiful or an ugly face. We are not a thin or a fat body. We are the soul or essence within.

Have you noticed that even though we see life around us wither, decay, and eventually die—even though we know this material form we live in is not permanent—we still feel unsettled at the thought of withering and dying?

While in India, I also heard a folk tale about the illusory nature of female beauty. It goes like this:

A man fell in love with a beautiful woman, and he tried to seduce her. But because the woman was wise, she refused his advances. When the man persisted, she told him that if he came to her home in one week, she would satisfy his desires.

During that week the wise woman took strong laxatives and emetics and continually passed stool and vomited into pots. Within a week she turned thin, pale, and unappealing. At the week's end, when the lusty man arrived at her door, he didn't recognize her. He asked the woman for the beautiful girl he desired, and she told him it was her. He refused to believe her. Finally, she convinced him that she was the young woman he had come to see, but that for his pleasure she had separated the ingredients of her beauty and stored them in special pots. If he wished, she said he could enjoy those "juices of beauty."

He eagerly begged to see and enjoy those juices, so the woman led him into the room where the pots of stool and vomit were stored. When she opened the pots, naturally he was disgusted and bewildered. Then the wise woman explained that this stool and vomit were the only missing ingredients of her beauty, and in that moment, she enlightened him about the illusory nature of form—physical beauty.

The story is an exaggerated and graphic example of the temporary nature of our bodies, of form, but there's a lot of truth revealed here.

Our obsession with not wanting to grow old and die; our obsession with wanting to control how we look and feel, and our sadness when we see our bodies change, are all natural and understandable if we're believing that the thing that's changing and getting old is the real us. What is permanent and constant is that deeper part of ourselves—the world of non-form, our spiritual essence which is not subject to change or death.

We have the option to see our physical decline as a cruel joke, or we can see it as an opportunity to turn in a different direction and understand the truth of what's really going on—to understand what's underneath all of this flesh and bone, all of the thinking we have about ourselves—this world of form. To begin to wonder: if I don't have my physicality to lean on, then what do I have? Who am I?

As I look back on my life, it's clear that what has gotten in the way of true confidence shining through—what has sometimes stopped me from speaking out or playing bigger in life—is my own personal, overly self-conscious, judgmental thinking about myself, and my strong identification with my physical form—all taking shape through the moment to moment experience of thought.

In other words, what gets in the way of our confidence is when we take our thoughts about ourselves too seriously; when we believe that the thing we see in the mirror that we sometimes like and sometimes don't like, is the real us.

There have been too many times when I've been overly self-absorbed and attached to thoughts about my physical looks, and overly preoccupied with what others might be thinking about me. And so it's no wonder that feelings of insecurity would get in the way of my ability to create and hinder my becoming more visible in the world. These have been the most uncreative and deadening times of my life. I truly believe that the women who are genuinely making their mark in the world—the women who are having the greatest impact with their work and relationships—are not preoccupied with a lot of thinking about their physical attractiveness. They are able to let it go, because their work and service to the world, and the quality of their relationships is far more important than any insecure feeling.

The sadness I sometimes feel about my own physical decline is normal and understandable. And yes, it does feel like a loss. But as cliché as it sounds, I am seeing myself in a more multifaceted way that is not limited to the physicality of youthful-looking skin or a thin body. It's an opportunity and invitation to get to that space within and reconnect with the wiser and ageless self that is me. When I engage in the world of form, I connect with my appearance. When I look to the world within, I learn more about my true self.

What This Lie Has Cost Me: There have been many opportunities that I've squandered and missed out on to be more public with my work—and all because I've been overly self-conscious and insecure about my looks. The times that I've preferred to hide away have been the most uncreative, lonely, and sad moments of my life. It has been a loss for the people I want to serve and help, and a loss to me for not showing the world who I really am.

What The Truth Tells Me: Who I really am is not this body. I am so much more. When I connect with that deeper part of me that exists beyond form, I am fearless and naturally confident.

Confidence is not, "They will like me."
Confidence is, "I'll be fine if they don't."

–Christina Grimmie

Reflection by Lana:

We've all felt the need or desire to please others at one time or another. It's perfectly normal to want to feel accepted and loved. We are social beings who thrive on connection. While everyone wants to be liked and to fit in, there's a big difference between the desire for acceptance and the habit of people-pleasing.

Some common habits of people-pleasers are:

An obsessive desire to be liked by others.

Difficulty acting assertive and speaking their minds.

Feeling wounded and hurt when criticized by others.

Acting based on what other people think of them.

Feeling great compassion and understanding of others, but not of themselves.

Where people-pleasers innocently experience emotional discomfort, however, is in misunderstanding the role that other people play in our psychological well-being. We can unwittingly experience a feeling of anxiety and insecurity by placing too much importance on the opinions of others.

My own experience as a people-pleaser came about while waiting for my college professor who was late showing up for class. Many of the students decided to leave, and I decided to take a walk in the building. As I approached an open office door, I heard a voice and recognized that it was my "missing" professor. I tentatively peered in and saw that she was talking on the phone. My movement caught her eye and she quickly hung up and asked if I had a question. I must have looked like a deer in the headlights as I attempted to explain why I was at her door, and I agonized over whether or not to mention the fact that she was late for class. I was worried that if I said anything about her not showing up, or if I said nothing at all, she would be upset with me. I didn't feel confident to simply state the facts to her.

I ended up saying nothing, rationalizing that most of the kids had already left. In reality, however, thoughts of disapproval, anger and insecurity flooded my mind. Not understanding the nature of thought and the mechanics of the mind, I took such thoughts personally and very seriously which ultimately left little room for a clear solution to surface. Ironically, as I returned to the lecture hall the professor arrived on my heels in a flurry. Noticing me she proceeded to verbally reprimand me for my negligence in not informing her that she was late. I felt both humiliated and angry at her and myself. If only I'd had the self-assurance to tell her about what had actually happened, knowing that no matter what her response, I would be okay.

Whatever she was feeling in that moment had nothing to do with me and everything to do with how thought was showing up and being experienced through her in that moment. It wasn't personal...for her or for me. Neither one of us understood this at that time, however.

I acted the way I did out of insecurity and a fear of reprisal for being the bearer of bad news. And being the consummate people-pleaser, I also didn't want to be responsible for causing her to feel upset—little did I know back then that this was totally out of my control.

And don't we all do this every day in some form or other?

We seem to go out of our way to play a role for each and every person that comes into our life, thinking that we'll avert their disapproval or anger. We become chameleons, shaping and shifting our moods, personalities, tones, demeanor, and voices so as not to offend or disappoint. Ultimately, however, we are left exhausted and depleted which only acts to feed our insecurity.

So often, we mistakenly tie our own feelings of confidence to how we believe others are thinking about us. Every interaction becomes an ordeal that either temporarily bolsters our confidence or diminishes it. And so we inadvertently hitch our feeling of confidence to an ever-moving goalpost that, in reality, doesn't even exist.

We *think* that by pleasing others we can control how they feel about us.

We *think* that by doing so, we will feel confident.

The above would be accurate except for one glaring *misunderstanding*:

Feelings are NOT derived by outside forces. They are exclusively an inside job.

Feeling insecure is simply insecure feelings being brought to life within the mind. It may feel connected to something or someone outside of us because we are so conditioned to look that way for an explanation for our feelings, but in reality, the feeling is always being brought to life within the mind. No exceptions.

That is why some days you can feel particularly insecure when someone seems displeased with you and other days it barely raises a feather.

While we may not like feelings of insecurity, when we understand where they are coming from, they don't look so scary. And... when we understand that feelings are experienced the same way for everyone, it no longer makes sense to try to twist ourselves into pretzels in an attempt to please others since we know that feelings come from within. You know the phrase, "there's no pleasing you!" It is based in truth. Our minds, however, try to convince us otherwise and keep us spinning in an endless circle. When we step out of the circle and understand how life is coming to us and everyone else in every moment, it no longer makes sense to try to control others in order to feel something within ourselves. That feeling we desired was never out there.

If I had of known this back then, I may have saved myself a lot of anxiety, especially when I was hired for my first real job. I was finally earning a salary for the first time in my life and I felt happy, confident, and excited about my position. A year later, a wonderful young man, who became my friend, was hired to do the same job as I was doing. I soon discovered, however, that he was earning one-third more money than I was. I was shocked and confused when I found out, and I was determined to rectify what I viewed to be an outright injustice.

Despite my intent to speak up, uppermost in my mind was the thought that if I were to complain and ask for equal pay, I may be viewed as pushy, greedy, entitled and ungrateful. My confidence wavered up and down as my mind worked through the various scenarios. I had mistakenly believed that confidence could be directly affected by the opinions of others. What I didn't know back then was that confidence is a quality that is innate within all of us when not obscured by insecure thinking.

So, if our confidence is not truly dependent upon the opinions of others, what do we do when we find ourselves getting caught up in a pattern of people-pleasing?

The good news is that we are designed to move in and out of our feeling states naturally. Functioning in life is not dependent on feeling confident *all of the time*. Moods fluctuate. *States of being* fluctuate. Thinking changes all the time. As a result, our experience of life is constantly changing. It is simply the nature of being alive and being human. We can feel insecure about how others are perceiving us, and still speak our minds, or say no to a request. When we know that a *feeling* merely reflects our *thinking* in the moment, we are less inclined to take it seriously and therefore less likely to attach more meaning to it. This allows our thinking to pass through us more easily.

More good news: Our feeling state is actually a gift. It acts to notify us of the quality of our thinking, so when we find ourselves saying *yes* when we mean *no*, AND we feel the burden of that decision, we're alerted that our thinking is not in alignment with our well-being.

But my thinking looks and feels so real!

It is designed to feel real. Consciousness brings to life our thinking through our senses. The more thinking we have about something, the more real and compelling it looks. And, it *is* real...or at least we experience it as real until we remember what thought is and how the mind works.

Feelings of insecurity can feel intense because they are being brought to life by consciousness which is like the most advanced special effects program in the world...

BUT...

Knowing that we are only ever experiencing thought and feeling in the moment and that it is created within the mind and designed to move through us...

Knowing that we are designed *to have insights* that return us to our wisdom and common sense…

Knowing that nothing outside of us has the power to make us feel anything…

Knowing that confidence is an innate quality that is only ever obscured by thought in the moment…

Knowing all of this, we can once again wake up to the nature of thought, how our experience of life is created and the brilliance of our design.

Nothing and no one, except our experience of thought in the moment, can obscure the presence of our confidence. Ever.

What This Lie Has Cost Me: Trying to please others began as an effort to keep me feeling safe. In doing so, however, I hurt myself. I unwittingly reinforced within me the notion that showing up as myself would somehow be disappointing to others and diminish my confidence. As if I could control or influence their opinion. Ultimately, my attempt to keep myself safe kept me in a near constant state of anxiety.

What The Truth Tells Me: I have no control over the opinions or emotional states of others. Period. How others experience me has everything to do with their own experience of thought in the moment. Knowing this changes the relationship I have with the idea of control. If I can't control how others perceive me, then they also can't control how I perceive them, or even how I perceive myself. That is true freedom.

Argue for your limitations and, sure enough, they're yours.
-Richard Bach

Reflection by Linda:

Have you ever noticed that you can feel confident in one situation but not in another? That depending on who you're around, your level of insecurity and confidence can soar or plummet?

When I was in graduate school, I could talk confidently for hours to a student friend about my ideas for a term paper, but put me in the same situation with my professor or a large group seminar, and I would clam up and feel as if I were back in grade school.

Once upon a time, I worked in the world of international development; I was actually a school teacher who at the time was unable to find a teaching position, and so I reluctantly accepted a job working as a project coordinator for a large non-profit organization. My boss was a wonderful, egalitarian woman, and the director of an international initiative on youth employment—it was a job that had the two of us traveling all over the world.

As her assistant, I regularly found myself sitting around a table with very high-level people to discuss our global initiatives. These distinguished participants were vice-presidents of the World Bank, Ambassadors at the United Nations, and world-famous scholars and researchers from various Ivy League schools. We even held a meeting at the British Commonwealth attended by prominent Members of Parliament.

I experienced a lot of anxiety at those meetings, and at the time, I believed it had a lot to do with the fact that the content of my work was not my field of expertise. After all, I was an English teacher, and I knew very little about the global issues of youth employment. That was one legitimate excuse I believed was the cause of my insecurity in this job. Another was that I felt out of my depth. I couldn't understand why I was being invited to give an opinion. The people at these meetings were way ahead of me in terms of the subject matter and professional status.

As I sat in those meetings, I'd wonder: "How the heck did I get here?" "Why was I invited to contribute?" I had a clear case of what we call *imposter syndrome*, and so I would sit in those meetings in abject fear, wondering when someone was going to discover that I actually didn't belong there; and I wondered how much longer I could get away with posturing in this way. I remember wishing that someone would call me on my phone so that I'd have to get up and leave the room. Sometimes, the pressure felt so great, and my feelings of insecurity became even more intense, that I would actually leave the room pretending to go to the restroom—anything to escape the possibility of being asked to give an opinion. I didn't care if it was obvious to everyone that I was opting out when it came time for me to contribute. Anything was better than worrying about what I was going to say or suffering the anguish and humiliation over what others would think of me.

We humans love to label our conditions—our insecurities—as a real THING. We like to be able to say: *I have imposter syndrome*, rather than just call it out for what it is: *I have a lot of insecure thinking going on right now*. For me, defining myself in this way kind of got me off the hook about showing up and contributing. But here's the amazing thing about all of this. I eventually discovered that my wonderful boss, had actually very little experience in international development. She had been a stay at home mom for most of her life, and had decided that once her kids were older, she would do something for the youth of the world. In fact, there were times when she confessed to me that she didn't really know how to proceed with this project—that she was depending on the goodwill and advice of her mentors and stakeholders to guide her in her decision-making. She also shared with me that she often felt scared, intimidated, and out of her depth when talking to people. She too had a case of *imposter syndrome*.

One thing that was eminently clear to me, was that my boss's ability to show up and contribute, despite her insecurities, was driven by her strong desire and passion to make a difference in the world. There were many times that I witnessed her go through moments of insecurity and in the next breath, see her get on with whatever had to be done.

And therein lies the difference between people who (innocently) back off and shrink themselves from showing up and who make it all about them (like me at the time), and people like my boss who refuse to let how they feel get in the way of something bigger than themselves.

You may be reading this and thinking that my fear was justifiable and reasonable—most English teachers know very little about international development. What contribution could I possibly offer?

But here's the odd thing.

Whenever my boss would convene roundtable meetings back at our office with my peers and our interns, I felt no dread. No fear. In fact, I looked forward to those meetings, because I was always in a relaxed "state of mind". And it was because of my relaxed state, that I found myself full of ideas that I expressed openly and confidently with others. Even at the risk of saying something of no value (which happened often), I was totally at ease either way.

It would seem that in both graduate school and at my job, my lack of confidence was because I was intimidated by high-level people, and it was when I was in those circumstances that I felt feelings of inadequacy. I was blaming and pointing to some circumstance—being around figures of authority, and having no background in the issues of youth employment—as the cause of my insecure thinking. But the truth was that I did have it in me to contribute. The ability was there. Confidence was there inside of me. I had proved it to myself over and over.

I can see now that my natural confidence was stifled and obscured by the busyness that was going on in my head. And that busyness was made up of lots of self-conscious thoughts about what was missing and lacking in me—it was all situation-specific. So instead of thinking about and concentrating on the content of the meeting—instead of being truly present—I was busy thinking:

What will they think of my comments?
Will they find my opinions laughable or silly?

Maybe they're wondering why I'm here in the first place.
What the hell am I doing here anyway?
I'm not in their league.
I feel like such an imposter—a phony.
Do I look the part? Is my outfit appropriate?
What if I can't think of anything to say?
I can't do this? How do I get out of here?

To illustrate how our insecurity has nothing to do with the situation at hand and everything to do with our thinking, imagine that you are speaking with a friend who you feel completely at ease within a large conference room. Now imagine that the room slowly begins to fill up as more people enter the room to hear what you have to say. At what point do you begin to get uncomfortable? When do you start to feel insecure and unable to think clearly? Can you see that something switched in your thinking about the situation?

When we have a head full of insecure thinking, when we're not relaxed, it's much more difficult to experience insights, clarity, or creativity. In fact, we actually inhibit our ability to be articulate, present, and maybe even original.

And here's the biggest irony: I can see now that my insecure thinking was ironically very much ego-driven. It became all about ME. *What will others think about ME? Will they think MY contributions are valid?* My ability to be truly present with other people was greatly diminished. I couldn't hear what they had to say because I was too focused on my own inner dialogue. And so, my lack of confidence was in a strange way, actually a preoccupation with myself, because I thought that everyone was focused solely on me.

But let's consider: What if I had been knowledgeable and accomplished in the area of international development, maybe even an expert, what then? Would that have guaranteed that I would have shown up confidently at those meetings? Not necessarily. There are many intelligent people who know their subjects well and yet who still suffer anguish from a lack of confidence.

Self-help books often emphasize that confidence comes from one's past accomplishments and experiences, in the same way that a muscle needs to be exercised to be made strong. And that the more we practice putting ourselves out in the world—the more we *feel the fear and do it anyway*, the more we *act as if*, the more we *consider our past accomplishments and successes*—that's when our confidence muscle will become robust and strong. This advice does work, but only up to a point.

If it were the case that exercising the muscle *alone* worked, then why would so-called confident people continue to experience a lack of confidence from time to time and allow it to get in the way of their work?

I have a friend who does a lot of public speaking. She speaks eloquently about her subject; she really knows her stuff. She's been *exercising* her confidence muscle for fifteen years, and yet she still doubts herself, she still has jitters before every talk, she still anguishes over giving a presentation, and she still occasionally gives a less-than-stellar performance.

The confidence that I wanted so badly in those meetings had very little to do with my knowledgebase, past experience of success, or expertise. My insecurity was all about the cluttered thinking I was carrying around in my head at that moment. I was the one who was innocently inhibiting my confidence from coming through. Confidence is always there within us.

We tell ourselves the lie that we can only be confident in certain situations—that the conditions have to be right. This is an example of *outside-in* thinking, or blaming external circumstances for how we feel and act. But it's never about external circumstances. No matter what the conditions, our level of confidence is a direct reflection of our thinking in the moment—whether we have a clear mind or not in that moment.

When I taught high school—the job I was trained to do—I was the kind of teacher that always over-prepared my lessons, but there were occasional days that I just didn't have the time to prepare. I remember feeling nervous and insecure about what I was going to say in class—if I didn't have a plan, how would I know what direction the class would go in? What if I didn't know what to say? But those unprepared classes turned out to be some of my best teaching experiences because I had no choice but to trust that something would show up, that wisdom would guide me in the right direction. Sometimes it didn't, but it nearly always did. When I found myself relaxed and didn't pay much attention to my mind, that's when we had some of our best classes.

Ultimately, confidence comes down to the amount of trust and certainty we have in understanding how the equipment of the mind works—that there is an unlimited supply of fresh new thought. It's not about self-help tools and gaining information—none of that ever led me or my clients to lasting and true transformation. It's not that we should dismiss our intellect or not prepare ourselves, or become skilled at something. We can do all of those things, but we can also relax into our wisdom. Our intellect is actually the servant to our wisdom.

Knowing what to say, or not to say—is always there within us. We can access it when we naturally find our solutions to problems by trusting how the system works. It has been proven to me over and over that there is a space within where confidence resides, and that it's as natural to me as knowing my own name.

What This Lie Has Cost Me: I missed out on being a valuable contributor at those meetings; and I suffered needless anxiety and wasted energy worrying about how others were seeing and reading me.

What The Truth Tells Me: I had the innate ability and confidence all along to contribute or not, to be brilliant or boring. And to be okay with whatever showed up.

A flower does not think of competing with the flower next to it.
It just blooms.

–Sensei Ogui

Reflection by Lana:

Comparing ourselves to others is a perfectly normal behavior. In fact, it seems a rather human thing to do. Sometimes we use comparison as a gauge to determine "how we're doing". In such cases, it can be helpful or motivating. At other times comparison can be counterproductive as it leads us down a rabbit-hole of despair, because we will always be able to find someone who is stronger, smarter, taller, shorter, kinder, or fitter...and on and on. The path of compare and despair leads to a bottomless pit.

Even though comparing ourselves to others can be helpful, the problem arises when we make such comparisons *mean* something about our own sense of worth—that's when we can experience a whole lot of unnecessary suffering for ourselves.

It's funny how we can so easily and mistakenly assume that others have it easier, or believe that they don't struggle with their own confidence at times. We have this notion that there are these perfect people out there living a yippy skippy life. Social media does a good job of reinforcing this assumption; it is the ultimate enabler, encouraging us to compare the raw reality of how we *feel* on the *inside* with the polished and selective versions of what we *see* in the lives of others on the *outside*.

And I have not been exempt from this.

They say that if you really want to know yourself—or rather, discover your "issues"—have a child or start a business.

45

Well, I've done both and I can honestly say that in both cases my "issues" were definitely brought to the forefront. For this chapter though, I'm going to focus on my efforts to start a coaching business.

As soon as I hung up my coaching shingle to let people know I was ready for business, I found myself comparing my progress and output to those of other more successful coaches. Even though I had mastered the skills of cognitive therapy, and even though I had an arsenal of tools and techniques under my belt, the compulsion to compare myself with others became a regular preoccupation and occurrence. I couldn't help but notice that other coaches had already written a book (or two); had created a catchy niche; or had developed compelling online programs.

Meanwhile, I was still stuck wondering who my ideal client was or what to offer, to say nothing of how to become more visible. It seemed as if other coaches had a real business, while I had a hobby. Instead of getting to work on my business, I would spend hours working on managing and manipulating my mindset; searching endlessly to find a "better-feeling thought", and I was forever waiting around for the inspiration to hit me so that I could take inspired action— anything that would end my misery of feeling inferior, inept, and deficient.

Let's face it. Some people are just better at doing certain things than others. That's the reality. And if we don't allow ourselves to accept this reality, we're never going to get off our butts and do something. But here's the thing: even those people who seem to be more successful than us, experience compare and despair days. And you can bet that if I were to look behind the scenes of those successful coaches that I wasted time envying, I'd discover that they too have days when they struggle to get out of bed and *seize the day* or don't always know what to do or what to write.

No one lives a life of perfection. None of us get to experience perfection. The only thing that is perfect is our true nature. And that perfection is made up of the ups and downs of life; the insecure days and the confident days; the tired days and the sprightly days; the sick days and the vibrant days; the creative days and the dull days. All of it. What is perfect is the whole beautiful messiness of being human. Just because someone can do something better than us, doesn't mean there is something wrong with us. Thinking about ourselves in this way is one of the biggest traps we can fall into, because our first response is to want to fix what we see as the problem.

Instead of getting on with growing my coaching practice, instead of spending my days creating and coaching; I wasted my time trying to make myself feel better and less self-conscious—I was forever 'working on myself'.

Do I still compare myself to others? Of course I do. We all do. The difference is that now I know where my feelings are coming from. I no longer attribute them to some truth about myself just because I experienced a thought that said so. I recognize the randomness of thought. And I realize that it is only when I take thought personally and confuse its *content* with *who I am* at my core, that I experience emotional or psychological suffering.

Thoughts are neutral. They come and go of their own accord. Hang onto them...believe them...take them to heart...and you can literally experience heaven or hell on earth.

The only constant to who we really are resides before thought. It is that deeper place beyond the intellect that is our default and is always there within us. It is where we find wisdom and clarity and confidence, and it's always present beneath our moment to moment experience of life. In this place, there is no desire or concern for comparison. It is irrelevant.

I now understand that I don't have to live up to anyone else's standards; and because of that, I don't have to spend a lifetime working and focusing on myself. Ironically, in releasing myself from this self-imposed pressure, I have reconnected with my creative confident core, and I've been able to show up and serve to the best of my ability.

So, let's all do ourselves a favor: Let's stop *working on ourselves*, and get on with whatever it is we want to create.

What This Lie Has Cost Me: By unwittingly funneling my energy into the compare/despair rabbit-hole of doom, I had very little energy left to focus on what I wanted to create and how I wanted to show up in the world. I was looking at others and what I thought I lacked rather than where I was and what I wanted to create.

What The Truth Tells Me: No-one has a perfect life. What is perfect is our ability to be human and show up as is.

A Prayer to those Who Compare

Oh life,
though I live long,
meaning forsakes my name
as I race to collect another reflection.
Though I am not and will not be the last to
breathe, stare, stand, and die on this planet,
I will do so in a way that is not replicable.
My limbs,
weak and strong
with need to hold what others do
and
walk with the ease that others do.
My eyes,
strong from use
as such muscles are used to look at others
and
back to a mirror.
My feet,
sore from walking
in an imitation of the shadow
of my heroes and heroines.
Though my body is weakened
with the strain of jealousy
I continue to stare
and
compare.
I race and wobble to be like them.
I pantomime holding their burdens and titles and mantles
as if imagining
will make it so.
There are times when I forget to look up
and I catch the sight of a shoe behind me.
I look back and see a younger person,
a child,
a friend,
a stranger,

trying in vain to copy my steps.
I desperately want to call out that I am not one to be envied.
I am merely
a shadow of the shadow of my heroes.
But I stay quiet.
I hold back this confession,
as I am no different.
I hear the same voice that keeps my eyes flickering
and my body in pursuit.
As a drug addict knows they worship poison,
I know what salvation could save me;
Breathe,
Be yourself,
for there is no value in living like a shadow.

-Ava Dickson, 17 years old

*If the only thing people learned was not to be afraid of their
experience, that alone would change the world.*

–Sydney Banks

Reflection by Linda:

As a coach, I cannot tell you how many women have shared that the reason they can't leave a 'bad' relationship is because they're afraid of living alone. Never mind the fact that they are miserable. The fear of living alone feels far worse than putting up with a crappy relationship.

This was a circumstance I knew really well. For my entire adult life, my insecurity had me believing that I could not live happily or thrive if I didn't have a man in my life. And so from the ages of eighteen to forty-five, I was either married or living with someone. My pattern was to drift on for years in unsatisfying relationships and only leave when I was sure I had another new one ready to jump into.

There's a wonderful metaphor I once heard that aptly describes how our ability to continue to put up with a '*shitty*' life is (appropriately) akin to sitting in a dirty diaper. We know it's uncomfortable, messy, and undesirable, but we continue to do it anyway.

I've personally sat in a lot of metaphorical dirty diapers throughout my life, and it's typically involved a lot of dysfunctional thinking about me and my relationships with men. I don't know what triggered me to start believing I couldn't survive without a man—maybe I read too many Grimm's fairy tales and Gothic novels as a young girl—but that's what happened. From a very early age, I got entangled in a web of thinking that convinced me my life wouldn't be complete unless I was in a relationship.

I used to believe that the thoughts that popped into my head had real significance and were true (except for the really wacky and surreal ones). Unbeknownst to me, I didn't know that my day-to-day experience was created *through* thought. And it was because of this misunderstanding that I ended up experiencing a lot of unnecessary fears and anxieties in the area of relationships.

Here's just one example:

I remember the day well. My live-in partner of ten years had packed his truck with his belongings. He was an electrician, and he'd decided to leave Boston and take a job in Chicago. Everything was arranged. Life with each other had become intolerable for many reasons. He was a decent, kind, and committed partner, but he was all wrong for me in so many other ways. I was definitely not in love. He had become a constant source of pressure and stress to me (and I to him).

So why then was I on my knees crying and begging him to stay? I considered myself a smart woman. I was well-educated, and I had a good job with a steady paycheck. But the thought of living on my own terrified me.

Never mind the fact that we were never happy or that all we did was fight with each other. Here was my opportunity to end this thing and to finally get him out of my life. But in that moment, on that day, I just couldn't do it. And so, after hours of crying and pleading, he unpacked his truck and agreed to stay.

It would take another three years of living with him—of continuing to sit in that 'dirty diaper'— to realize once again that he was all wrong for me. But the day finally did come when I *knew* for sure that I had to get out.

When you've been thinking your whole adult life that living without a partner is something to be feared and avoided, it's not a belief you can suddenly change. A belief that's inhabited your head for thirty years (as was my case), has a lot of momentum going for it. It becomes your identity.

I had been sinking in a swamp of thoughts that convinced me I was incomplete without a man. And with it came a lot of other fearful thoughts such as: *How can I cope financially on my own? How will I deal with the loneliness? Who is going to take care of me? Who am I without a man?*

Other women could stand on their own two feet. But not me. In the same way that we label ourselves as British, introverted, shy, Caucasian, I

52

had labeled myself with an indelible stamp as someone who had no confidence or resiliency to make it alone.

As I look back on that time, I am amazed (and saddened) at how my life was dictated and driven by this belief. If only I had known that all of that thinking about my need for a man was just that: THINKING.

Many years later, when I hired a coach, I told her how insecure I felt about living on my own. And then she said something to me that really ticked me off:

"But Linda, that's just a thought you're thinking".

It was the first time I'd ever heard anyone talk about thoughts and thinking, as if they were separate from me. Her comment annoyed me because it seemed as if she was making light of *my thought* and *my experience*. She couldn't truly be listening, I rationalized, since it felt like my experience was being reduced to *just a thought*. I wanted my experience to have great meaning, significance, and importance. I wanted it to be a big thing. I wanted her to dive into my swamp and feel what I was feeling. Because guess what? I believed I *was* my thinking.

I have come to understand that thoughts come into our mind of their own accord. Some stand out more than others; some get our attention. Some of them goad us into playing with them. Some want to be validated and respected, and never ignored. There are some thoughts we get intimate, cozy and warm with. We feed them. We become great listeners. We engage in deep dialogue. And we risk getting entangled in a web of sadness, melodrama, fear, insecurity, and a host of other dark and heavy emotions. Such is the seduction of thought.

Thought is like clay in the way that anything can be made of it. For me, I had made an identity of myself as an insecure woman unable to live without a man. I didn't know that thought was just like clay—that I either made something of, or not. I didn't know that thoughts would move on and out of my life naturally. My feelings of insecurity had been made out of thought. My feelings of fear had been made out of thought. It had all been made up and yet I had built my life around it. And like an undesirable roommate, those insecure thoughts moved in, took over, and created havoc and confusion in my life.

My decision to leave was way overdue because I didn't know or understand that I was the thinker, making up my decisions moment to moment. I didn't know back then that a thought would occur and that I didn't have to believe it and let it define or dictate my life. I didn't know that if I left my insecure thoughts alone, they would move on all on their own, and in so doing, a space would be created—a space for new thoughts to show up and guide me towards what's really true about my ability to be resilient and confident.

It amazes me that for almost forty years, I believed that life with a man was the thing that would make my life better—a man was the solution to my loneliness and insecurity. You couldn't convince me otherwise. Life with a man was how I self-medicated, and it got in the way of me connecting with myself on a deeper level. I had never allowed myself the inner space to connect with my true self; I kept filling that space with a man. This dependence and need for something outside of us to make us feel whole is one of the biggest misunderstandings we have about what allows us to experience wholeness and happiness in life. It's us just experiencing life from the *out-side-in*.

I find it interesting that in the early days of my relationship, my head was full of *I can't live without him*, thoughts. And then when I finally decided to leave, my head was full of *I'm going to break his heart*, thoughts. And then when I finally discovered that I could make it on my own, I had thoughts of *living alone can be fun*, and *I'm actually going to be OK*. Throughout our lives, we experience a never-ending supply of thoughts that we interpret as both "good" and" bad". What I've come to realize is that it's not *thought* that got me into trouble, but my misunderstanding of how the system was working through me.

When the electrician and I finally separated, I remember walking into my empty apartment for the first time after a long day at work. I felt some of the old habitual, fearful thinking, worrying how I was going to survive on my own. Those old thoughts were lingering and waiting to be let in again, wanting to warm up and get cozy with me like they did in the old days. And as I stood in my half-empty apartment, those thoughts hung around for a while, and then they seemed to evaporate into the air and were overshadowed by a series of thoughts that left me with a giddy feeling of freedom. And for the first time, I heard some new, fresh thinking. I knew that I was going to be okay. That even though I would feel those old insecure feelings from time to time, I knew that I was okay.

What This Lie Has Cost Me: I spent years feeling anxious and fearful about making sure I had a man in my life, not knowing or believing that I would be OK without one if I chose; and because of this—because I never put myself first—I never allowed myself at that time to know who I really was and what I was capable of achieving on my own. All of this happened due to a misunderstanding of how thought was creating my experience.

What The Truth Tells Me: I had everything I needed, even without a man. I had the ability to survive, even thrive, without a man.

We insist on being Someone, with a capital S. We get security from defining ourselves as worthless or worthy, superior or inferior. We waste precious time exaggerating or romanticizing or belittling ourselves with a complacent surety that yes, that's who we are. We mistake the openness of our being – the inherent wonder and surprise of each moment – for a solid, irrefutable self. Because of this misunderstanding, we suffer.

–Pema Chodron

Reflection by Lana:

We've all experienced our own version of not feeling '*good enough*'. For some of us, it may be not feeling smart enough. For others, not rich enough, or not outgoing enough. For me, it was simply that I was *overall*, not enough; that somehow deep in my core, I was lacking—and if people really got to know me they would also see this in me.

When I look back, I can see that my feelings of not being 'good enough' began in my childhood years and, like the origin of most strongly held beliefs about ourselves and our worth, there is usually one particular incident that stands out from the rest. And it's at this tender age, we make a decision about ourselves and our worth.

Before I share my own story, let me preface it by saying that, as a parent, I am only too aware (and unaware) of any number of "*mistakes*" I've made with my own children. I am also aware of how easily these mistakes can be made without any intention to do so. After all, we only experience life one way; through the filter of our own thinking.

What I also now know to be true is that people do the best they can given their own thinking. There is no blame here. There is only room for understanding, love, and compassion for the parties involved.

What I now understand to be true is that NO ONE can take away *my* wholeness, just like NO ONE can take away *your* wholeness. My issue of feeling "not good enough" was a figment of my imagination that I innocently bought into. I just didn't know any better. Like most kids, I looked up to my parents as god-like creatures and as such, their words and actions had an impact on my perceptions of the world and of myself. I misunderstood, however, some fundamental truths about thought and experience.

So, here is my story as I experienced it at the time:

When I was five years old, I was hit by a bike on our street. When my father learned what had happened, he put me on the handlebars of his bike and rode around the neighborhood trying to find the man who had knocked me over. It was the first time I remember feeling truly loved and protected by my father. It was perhaps the only time. I cherished that memory for years and conjured it just for the feeling of being loved by him. Funny how such memories stick with you.

For much of my life, it was that memory that I used to offset many of my other not so good memories.

My father was born in the northern part of Italy during World War II and had emigrated to the United States as a teenager. He is a highly educated man who went on to become a professor. It was, therefore, with much pride that my father took his American wife and two young daughters to Italy to meet his family.

My mom, sister, and I felt like fish out of water during that trip. Not being able to understand or speak Italian, we felt awkward and tried to smile while meeting my father's uncle. Taking us aside, my father looked at us sternly and said, "My uncle thinks you are cold and unfriendly". I was shocked and hurt. What do you say after something like that? What do you do? I didn't say anything. I simply tried to make myself smaller as I watched my father laugh with his uncle, leaving the three of us huddled together on our own. I was hurt that my father had not defended or reassured us at the time. I even wondered why he chose to translate his uncle's impression of us. Did he not think it would hurt us? I will never know. What I do know, however, is that it was at *that* moment that something *appeared* to be confirmed within me; I believed that my father found us *lacking*.

In my child's mind, I came to the conclusion that something was fundamentally wrong with us...*with me*. Somehow we weren't enough for him; *I wasn't enough. If my own father can't love me unconditionally, or doesn't feel inclined to protect me against such harsh judgement, then who would?*

From that point on, I unconsciously and consciously collected the evidence that would cement my conclusion; *I am not enough as I am*. It's true what they say, "*Seek, and ye shall find*". For in my search, I found mountains of evidence *everywhere*...every look, every word, every nuance, every silence, gesture, sigh, mood, action, inaction...all of it pointed to the 'fact' that I was lacking in the eyes of my father.

It came as no real surprise, then, when my father announced that he would be teaching summer school in Italy for the next few years without us. It just so happened that my birthday coincided with his absences, and so year after year, he would miss my birthday. While I was promised a celebration upon his return, it never really came to pass, and any attempt to make it happen was half-hearted, at best (more evidence). Year after year, I held out hope that somehow he would do something special for me from Italy. Year after year it was the same. Nothing. My belief in my "lacking" solidified even more as every year my birthday became emblematic of this lacking.

If my own father seemed unwilling to acknowledge the day of my birth in some special way, then I must indeed be lacking.

On another trip to Italy, I was secretly thrilled that my family was finally all together, and it just so happened to coincide with my thirteenth birthday. This was IT, I thought. No more excuses. The time was ripe for my own redemption.

My parents decided we'd all go out for dinner that night, and as we ate, I kept glancing around hoping for something special to happen, something that would finally assure me of my official *worth* in their eyes. Sure enough, shortly after our plates had been cleared a beautiful birthday cake emerged from the kitchen! I was ecstatic. Not only had they remembered, but they had planned something special *just for me*. Smiling broadly, I blew out the candles and eagerly accepted a piece of cake. MY cake...which, in my mind at the time, categorically symbolized the special place I held in their hearts, just as I was. As I bit into the cake, however, I realized that it was *full* of alcohol. This wasn't a cake for a kid. This was a cake for adults. I was crestfallen as I pushed my plate to the side. My old belief came roaring back to life.

I must be lacking in something if my own parents felt it more important to arrange for a cake that they would enjoy rather than one I could eat.

After that, it seemed as if evidence of my *not being good enough* was everywhere, and I began to develop a protective wall of false confidence wherever I could (never let 'em see you sweat, was my motto). What I didn't understand at that time, or for many years after, was that I had erroneously latched onto a thought ("not good enough") and created an identity around it.

Because I believed that only my father could bestow a "good enough" value onto me, I began an exhausting search for his approval. I mistakenly thought that I needed *him* to make me feel that I was *good enough*. To me, it all seemed so obvious that something *outside* of me—my family and the events that had occurred—were the cause of why I felt the way I did. They had the power to make me feel a certain way. Right?

Little did I know, at the time, that I was innocently looking in the wrong direction for solace, peace and comfort. I was looking in the direction of continued pain and suffering. And as natural as it was to see my father as responsible for how I felt, my young self didn't know that the only thing I can feel in any moment is the product of the thinking I am entertaining at that time. If only I had of known that just because I have a thought, it doesn't mean it's true—I had innocently believed otherwise. I believed that a cake had the power to make me feel a certain way, and that the actions of another person had the power to diminish my worthiness.

Fundamental worthiness is not something that can be increased or decreased by anyone else. Worthiness is a birthright and a constant, like the sun in the sky. Regardless of the clouds and the rain and the sleet and the snow, the sun is always present. Our worthiness is also always present even though it can appear to be obscured by the *weather of our thoughts*.

The challenge we often face is one of perceived relativity. As Einstein once explained, "Put your hand on a hot stove for a minute, and it seems like an hour. Sit with a pretty girl for an hour, and it seems like a minute." So it can seem with our thoughts. Uncomfortable feelings derived from uncomfortable thoughts can appear disproportionately prevalent and enduring *relative* to thoughts that appear neutral or even pleasant to us.

You may be thinking: *That's all well and good, but what do we do when our feelings are so strong, and it truly feels as if we aren't good enough?*

Until we get an insight or some fresh new thinking that awakens us to the fact that we are only experiencing the energy of *Thought* in the moment, and that it will pass much like a weather storm, there is not much we can do. Just by understanding that *thought* IS continually moving through us and creating our experience and recognizing that there is a place within all of us that is stable and true and remains unblemished by thought, goes a long way toward seeing our *not good enough* thoughts as just that—*thought*.

Think of a time, for example, when you've experienced a feeling of peace. Perhaps it occurred when you were out for a walk, sitting with your pet, laughing with friends, looking up at the stars, or involved in a project.

It doesn't really matter when or how it happened; just notice that when it does happen, you are more present and engaged with life. Notice how during such times, thoughts move in and out of you effortlessly and you feel no need or desire to attach to them, to personalize them, or to take them too seriously.

That is where we see our design in perfect balance; experiencing life moment to moment through thought and consciousness. In such moments, there is no lack. There is just a present awareness of life in all of its beauty, exactly as it is. Effortlessly, qualities of connectedness, love, creativity, compassion, confidence and contentedness naturally emerge. When we reflect on this, we realize that there was nothing that we *had to do* to bring these qualities forward. There were no thoughts we had to consciously *manufacture* in order to experience these qualities. They were already there, *within us* the whole time.

So, why don't we experience these qualities more often?

In a word, *thought*.

While our ability to think is an amazing instrument when it is understood, it can also be an instrument for self-inflicted frustration and psychological suffering. Given an initial distressing thought or situation, like the one with my father's uncle in Italy, we can find ourselves ruminating on that one thought...expanding and intensifying it in the process until all we can see and feel is what we've imagined within our mind's eye.

Thoughts are masterful at creating a world which imagines itself to be real.

Thoughts and our nature are like warm breath on a cold window pane. Breathe on the same spot without pause and the glass remains foggy and unclear. Leave space between breaths, however, and the glass returns to its natural state, allowing us to see clearly once again.

And so it is with our minds.

Ruminate and expand on the same distressing thought without pause, such as the thought, "I'm not good enough" and the mind becomes fogged and lacking in clarity.

Quite often, once we become aware that our lens is fogging, a space naturally emerges within the mind that no longer feels inclined to hold onto such repetitive thoughts. In this way, such thoughts naturally fall away permitting new thought and insights to occur which then create a different experience.

True magic and freedom from insecurity lay within my mind all along. But the game of life, such as it is, means that we sometimes fall asleep to our true and powerful nature and then wake up to it through insight...over and over again. The good news is that we are designed to wake up and that everything we seek for ourselves actually resides within.

While I still have moments of not feeling 'good enough', and thinking that something or someone *outside* of me can determine my worth, I can usually catch myself at some point and effortlessly find myself returning to a place of well-being that has only ever been obscured by thinking in the moment. My first clue tends to be the feeling of tension within my mind or body. That tension signals that I am not using my intellect wisely. I've also learned to recognize that the past will let go of me when I let go of it; I am the one innocently bringing it back to life through the power of thought.

Today I can see more clearly that my father is simply living his own experience of life via his thinking in the moment. It truly has nothing to do with me. As such, I can love him exactly as he is and know that beyond his own thinking he loves me exactly as I am.

Understanding the role of thought, and the nature of our personal minds to create a story from thought, goes a long way to revealing the truth of who we really are.

Our identity and our worthiness are separate. One is created within the mind moment to moment and the other just *is*...regardless of thought. There is nothing lacking.

> *"Boy, are you ever going to laugh when you discover you were perfect all along."*
> —*The Universe*

What This Lie Has Cost Me: Believing that my worthiness was something that had to be earned, cost me my peace of mind and ramped up my level of insecurity and for a while, obscured the love I felt for my father.

What The Truth Tells Me: There is nothing for me to prove or justify. I am. That is and always will be enough.

*I found that things became a lot easier when I am no longer
expected to win. You abandon your masterpiece and sink into
the real masterpiece.*

–Leonard Cohen

Reflection by Linda:

I have bowed my head in churches, mosques and temples. I've prayed,
chanted, and sung in choirs. I've read spiritual texts, hundreds of self-help
books, and a lot of Shakespeare. I've travelled to the foothills of the Hima-
layas where the Beatles meditated with the Maharishi Mahesh Yogi. And
there were years when I abstained from eating anything that had a face on
it.

My well-meaning attempts at becoming a better, purer, powerful,
enlightened, and more self-assured person have been ongoing and varied,
to say the least. But never in my wildest dreams would I have thought
that working for myself in my own business would end up being the
vehicle and catalyst that would finally expose my deepest fears and
insecurities about screwing up in public.

Let me explain...

As a personal development coach I've had some of the best training
from some seasoned, top-notch coaches, and alongside that, I've also had to
learn how to become a business person— how to let the world know that I
exist and what I have to offer.

And there's the rub.

That journey hasn't been easy. In fact, I've had some pretty dark days
where I've thought about closing up shop, and where the idea of a regular

job with a regular paycheck—a job where I could stay in the background, work behind the scenes—began to look like heaven. In short, I've had days where I would have given anything to get this entrepreneurial monkey off my back.

So what has all of this got to do with becoming a confident and more self-assured person? Well, almost everything. Because as I stumbled along this entrepreneurial path, I began to discover a lot about myself. And let me tell you, it wasn't all pretty.

I discovered that I have an endless loop of self-critical chatter going on in my head forever intent on reminding me that I'm not good enough or smart enough to be my own boss. There's the jealousy and envy ("compare and despair") that I feel toward other coaches who are more popular, make more money, and who appear more successful than I am. There's the inertia and lack of tenacity that I succumb to far too easily when I can't figure out how to do a technical task.

And here's the big one:

There's the fear I hide behind when I think about putting myself out into the world, because I've convinced myself that I'm not ready, not professional enough, not confident enough, not dynamic enough, not informed enough to launch myself. Yep, it's the fear of being judged—the fear of *what if I screw up in public along the way?*

Indeed, like many women who hold themselves back from going public with their work, I've suffered for years (and occasionally still do), believing that I'm too insecure to survive a public screw-up. In fact, one of my biggest fears is to appear unprofessional.

No-one in their right mind wants to screw up in public, but hey, welcome to the real world—it happens to all of us at some time. And guess what?

We ultimately ALWAYS survive it.

But for some of us, we may take longer to get over ourselves once we've gone through the humiliating experience of being caught with *spinach in our teeth*.

Here are two examples to illustrate a day in the life of someone (a famous person) who experienced what could be construed as a big humiliation, and who snapped out of it; and someone else (me) who ended up suffering for years because of one embarrassing incident.

I heard this story recently on the radio in an interview with the singer Judy Collins, and it really spoke to this issue of allowing ourselves to be okay with our public screw-ups:

Back in the mid-1960's, Judy Collins had a friend that she felt showed great promise and talent as a singer-songwriter. Once, when she was giving a concert, she invited him to join her on stage to sing his latest song. His name was Leonard Cohen.

At that time (according to Collins), Cohen had no experience as a singer, played guitar badly, and had never sung in public. But Collins knew his poems and songs were special and so she encouraged him on stage. Halfway through his performance, Cohen was so overcome with insecurity and self-doubt that he stopped his performance and walked off stage. Judy excused herself to her audience, went after him and told him that he had to go back and finish the song; that he couldn't leave it unfinished. And in that moment, despite his embarrassment and self-doubt, he walked back on stage and finished his performance.

The song he sang, *Suzanne*, went on to become an international hit, and his highly successful music career was launched.

I'll come back to Cohen, but first here's my story about screwing up in public:

Many years ago, when I worked as a high school English teacher, I attended a parent-teacher meeting. During that meeting the principal called on me, out of the blue, to say a few words to the parents about the benefits of students studying Shakespeare. Because I was completely caught off-guard, I lost my composure in that moment. I remember feeling intense anxiety about what I could possibly say that would impress those parents, teachers, and the principal. I was suddenly ensconced in a bubble of self-conscious thinking, believing everyone was looking at me to say something wonderful. After all, aren't English teachers meant to be good with words?

I was so overcome by the whole incident that I was unable to think clearly and put a coherent sentence together. To this day, I can't remember what I mumbled, but I do know that in that moment, I wanted to disappear. I convinced myself that, without a doubt, my reputation and I were forever ruined.

The incident was a defining moment for me because, for many years after, I would continue to feel anxious at public meetings, fearing that I would be called on to speak. I would purposely hide out and sit at the back of the room to avoid any situation in which I could be called on to give an opinion. I also felt increasingly intimidated whenever the principal would stop by and observe my class—he had an annoying habit of walking in unannounced. It would take me years to shake off the humiliation and emotional fall-out of that incident.

The embarrassment I felt was actually perfectly normal and under-standable—after all, don't we all want to be brilliant, articulate, and make a good impression in front of others? But the reality is that sometimes we're just not at our best. We are all going to have moments when we screw up, look silly, lack clarity, and experience humiliation. It's just a normal occurrence that everyone experiences at some time in their life. It's all part of being human.

I wasn't able to permit myself to be okay with my screw-up that day, and instead I chewed on my insecure thinking much longer than was necessary. I could have allowed myself to feel disappointed, chalked it up to a lack of experience, and moved on. I could have been a lot gentler and kinder to my young self and used the incident as an opportunity to be better prepared next time. Heck, I could have laughed it off.

Psychologist Dr. Steven Hayes, who is the pioneer of a therapy called "Acceptance and Commitment Therapy", has identified two types of emo-tional pain. He calls them *clean pain* and *dirty pain.*

"*Clean pain*" is when we naturally feel the pain of a bereavement, a relationship breakup, the loss of a job, an accident, or ill health, or in my case, the embarrassment of not being able to speak articulately when called upon. There's a natural cause and effect, and "clean pain" has a limited shelf-life. We experience the emotion, and then it naturally subsides over time.

Unfortunately, my response that day didn't take that *clean* path, because I added yet another heavy layer of thinking onto what was already perceived as an uncomfortable situation. I was deep in "dirty pain". "*Dirty pain*" occurs when we make up a *story* about our experience—we add meaning to the incident that it never really had. Layer upon layer of 'negative' thinking led me to a deep belief that I was, in fact, defective and just not good enough. I went from *clean pain* to *dirty pain* in a moment—and it's in the thick of that *dirty pain* that we really suffer and get stuck in an erroneous understanding of who we really are and what has happened to us.

Dirty pain comes from our thoughts about that situation or event. Something happens and rather than just deal with it and let it pass, we start spinning all manner of stories about it in our minds and make it more than it is.

Can you see how too much thinking—and in my case, too much self-conscious thinking—can cause us to go off track and end up in an undesirable mental space for longer than we want? Discomfort that could have lasted for a few hours or days ended up distorting my opinion about myself and giving me the excuse to feel and act small well after the fact. From that moment and for many years later, I defined myself as an insecure and professionally incompetent person.

Babies don't do *dirty pain*. They experience pure unadulterated thought that passes right through them. They are a good example and reminder of how we all started out in life and what our natural state is really like. Watch any baby. One moment they are crying their hearts out, and the next they're laughing.

When we were babies we "screwed-up" all the time. In our early attempts to eat food, we would get more food on our clothes and on the floor than in our mouths—it took us years to get it right, until we did. And yet, our parents (at least, healthy parents!) never ever thought badly about us or humiliated us. When babies are learning to eat their food, they do not naturally think:

Everyone's laughing at me because I can't hold a spoon.

Babies don't make their failure or mishaps mean something 'negative' about themselves, and they don't, in that moment, decide that they are forever an incapable and insecure person who can't find their way to their mouth. They cry and wail out their clean pain. They let the emotion pass through them, and then go back to being a happy baby that continues to screw up.

As I reflect back on my thoughts at school that day, I realize that I was convinced that everyone was intently focused on ME and the blunder I had made, when in fact they probably couldn't have cared less about me and my inability to speak.

I can now see that my feelings of insecurity were ironically me being in a state of self-absorption. I was making it all about ME. My way of coping with my problem was to find a way to fix the problem—to find a way to remedy the part of me that was incompetent and unprofessional. Thus began a long journey that would have me reading endless self-help books which I thought would help me analyze and dig deep as to why I was insecure.

My attempts led me to a myriad of self-development theories and strategies, which only resulted in me feeling even more entangled in my perceived problem. Little did I know back then, that it was only my relationship to my thinking that was the problem. Most of us don't realize that we are thinking our way through life—that we are making up our lives moment to moment. And how do we do this? Of the sixty-thousand-odd thoughts that we think every day, we give some thoughts more attention than others.

We latch on to some thoughts in the same way we latch on to the ticker tape news that runs along the bottom of our TV screen while watching a show, or the hundreds of Facebook feeds we scroll through every day. Some thoughts, some threads, or some news, just appeals to us more than others. Some scare us more than others. Some light us up. Some have no impact whatsoever.

Knowing how the "equipment" of my mind works would have been a huge game-changer for me at that time. Because what I didn't know back then, was that the busyness of my mind—my endless thinking about what's wrong with me and what to do about it—was actually the very thing that caused me to be stuck in my insecure state for many years following.

What I didn't know was that the mind has a built-in self-correcting system that is designed to move us towards balance, well-being, and clarity. And that self-correction happens automatically in the same way that clouds automatically move on their own accord. All I had to do was get out of the way and allow the mechanics of the mind to function as it was designed to do.

You may not be completely buying into the comparison that our thoughts move on in the same way that clouds move through the sky. After all, there's a big difference in thinking, *I shouldn't have bought those red shoes*, to a thought that's been with us for a long time and which may have included trauma, such as the one I carried for many years: *I'm not professional or smart enough.* For sure, these two thoughts are radically different, and in no way am I making light of despairing thoughts. But let's look closer at the weather metaphor. Aren't there times when the weather can be just as severe and harsh? When a hurricane passes through, we can lose our homes, belongings, our hope, and our life. And it's in these moments, when we're in the midst of the catastrophe, we feel the despair over what is happening.

But the truth is whatever weather we are experiencing is transitory by nature, and the blue sky will emerge once again because it never actually goes away—it just gets temporarily obscured. The stormy weather moves on and out without us having to do anything. We know that we just have to sit it through because mother nature is constantly changing and always returns to a state of balance and order.

When we experience our "human weather" it is because thought is moving through us. The difference is that we sometimes have a compulsion to hang out and get overly concerned about certain thoughts. We also have a strong impulse to want to do something about those thoughts or dig into the content of our thoughts.

In the same way that the sun and blue sky is the default and natural setting for the sky, we also have a default setting of innate well-being and a resilience which enables us to bounce back and not get stuck in our moods and fears.

In the same way that we can plug in an electrical appliance to make it work for us, our system can plug in or activate any thought to give it power, or not. When I had my parent-teacher experience that day, I not only decided that screwing up was something I would never survive, but I also innocently plugged in my insecure thinking.

Back to Leonard Cohen:

I would love to have known what actually happened to Cohen in that moment when he decided to go back on stage and finish his song. What went through his head? I imagine there's a strong possibility that the embarrassing and insecure thoughts he had experienced became unplugged which allowed his *clean pain* to move through him without spinning it into *dirty pain*.

Maybe in that moment he had the insight that his experience of insecurity and embarrassment wasn't happening *to him*, but coming *through him* via thought. Or that his feeling of self-consciousness wasn't that important. Because somehow or other, unlike me, he had the wherewithal not to take himself too seriously, to not make it so damn personal, to put his ego aside and allow a new thought to come through—a thought that was full of possibility and excitement. Or maybe he had the thought: *So what? So what if I screwed-up?* Cohen's experience is a powerful example of how our relationship with and our understanding of thought—a new thought—can lead us into some pretty amazing places in life—just consider Cohen's life.

There are going to be times in life when someone or some incident will trigger feelings of insecurity. Other people will laugh or criticize us and think our work isn't good enough. My own professional journey as an author and coach continues to remind me that it's okay and even necessary, to screw up if I ever want to evolve and put stuff out in the world—that I don't have to spend years recovering from my mistakes. It's not the failure that is significant—it's the belief that we won't be able to handle it that matters.

Instead, I could continue to stand there like a baby all naked and exposed—never pushing myself too hard, because I'll know that despite my blunders and my screw-ups, despite all of the embarrassing moments that will come along, I can survive and recover from all of it in a moment. This is the true meaning of confidence.

What This Lie Has Cost Me: For most of my professional life I believed that I wasn't competent, professional, or good enough. So much energy went into making sure never to put myself in a position where I would risk feeling the shame of screwing up in public. So much hiding, and so much effort to keep the beach ball under the water. So much work to feel safe.

What The Truth Tells Me: Everyone screws-up—especially people that put themselves out in the world. It's human to screw up, and it's actually mostly the way that we learn. We are all brilliant, and the only thing that gets in the way of us experiencing that is the insecure thinking we insist on holding onto and keeping alive.

*The woman who does not require validation from anyone is
the most feared individual on the planet.*

-Mohadesa Najumi

Reflection by Lana:

How many of us live in fear of being criticized? At the very least, few of us *enjoy* being criticized. Listen to any parent and undoubtedly you will hear them lament that they wish they could protect their child from the hurts and disappointments that come from being criticized.

But even that premise suggests a misunderstanding by parents because it is based on the common and pervasive belief that life is experienced from the *outside-in*. In other words, stuff *outside* of us causes us to feel something *inside*. After all, isn't it logical to point *outside* of ourselves toward the actions, words, and the demeanor of others to explain why we are *feeling*, *thinking* and *reacting* in the way that we do?

I once attended a party where I knew no one apart from the host. As I approached a group of women, I noticed that their loose circle began to imperceptibly close, giving me a clear message that I was not welcome. I remember feeling embarrassed, as if I had been sized up, judged and dismissed. In that instant, I reached the conclusion that something was wrong with me, and I responded accordingly—I turned tail and ran. Wouldn't anyone? Perhaps. But not everyone would have come to the same conclusions or taken the same actions.

What does this tell us?

It tells us that how we respond and interpret the events of our life, may have more to do with us than the event itself. In other words, my experience at the party illustrates how *I* was the one who decided in that moment that the women in that group were not interested in me being part of their group. And because of *that*, I created a story of rejection and humiliation. In effect, we are never *directly* experiencing any person or circumstance *as it is*. We are only ever experiencing a *personalized version* based on the thoughts and feelings we are having *about* the outside world within our minds.

So, if that is the case, why do we internalize criticism so deeply?

To help explain this, let's look at the Broadway musical *Chicago*, and one scene in particular. For those unfamiliar with the musical, it tells the story of the 1924 trials of two female murderesses who become enamored with their own fame and celebrity and engage a lawyer by the name of Billy Flynn to razzle and dazzle the jury in order to gain their acquittal. During one of the musical numbers, Billy Flynn explains exactly how he will secure their freedom. He sings,

"Give 'em the old Razzle Dazzle
Razzle dazzle 'em
Give 'em a show that's so splendiferous
Row after row will crow vociferous
Give 'em the old flim flam flummox
Fool and fracture 'em
How can they hear the truth above the roar?"

In other words, engage in a series of distractions that serve to overpower and overwhelm the *truth*. Be loud and outrageous and most certainly righteous in your claim...so much so that the *truth* becomes invisible to the jury. As audience members, we can see exactly what is going on; we see the manipulation and flagrant mishandling of the truth. We see the seduction of the jury and we wonder...

How can they be fooled? How can they not see the truth behind all of the noise?

Actually, quite easily. And this is exactly what happens within our own minds every single day.

Consider the number of times we've unwittingly listened to the loud, razzle-dazzle, outrageous and most certainly righteous claims within our own heads that say we're not good enough, smart enough, good-looking enough, rich enough, educated enough, tall enough, fit enough, funny enough, quick enough, articulate enough...enough, enough, enough.

Like the jury, we become seduced by the noise, distracted by its incessant chatter and apparent sincerity. We innocently assume that the loudest voice with the most razzle-dazzle (in the form of evidence from our past and emotional state of our present), deserves the most consideration.

All at once we become just like the jury in *Chicago*, overwhelmed by our very own internal Billy Flynn.

In the world of self-help there's a lot of talk about the *inner critic*—the 'nasty' voice in our head whose job appears to be criticizing our every move. We've all heard that voice and have innocently kept it alive by listening to it and believing it.

We can even begin to create habitual ways of thinking over time that create automatic neural pathways within our brain. We begin to *think* we *are* the criticisms we have internalized; that we are shy and insecure, withdrawn and quiet. We begin to behave and respond in ways that become automatic. And in a way, they are.

I've spent years trying to tame or stifle my inner critic. The self-help books even advised me to personalize it by giving the voice a name; engage in conversations with it for the purpose of telling it to be quiet; and I've spent endless hours trying to analyze why I believe the messages it gives me, revisiting my past to find the source of the messages I hear. But doing that only made me focus on the insecure thoughts more—what you see is what you get.

Here's the good news though: we need not be wedded to habitual patterns of thinking and being. There is a way out.

It was only a few years ago that we believed our brains were rigid in their ability to create new neural pathways—new ways of thinking. However, recent research has discovered that our brains retain a high degree of plasticity—the ability to reorganize and change throughout our lives. This is great news for us as it corroborates what anecdotal experience has illustrated for years. In simplistic terms, our mind is capable of experiencing insight that comes to us not from our brain power, but rather from a place deeper within all of us. It is the stable backdrop that acts to guide us invisibly and helpfully through life. We call it wisdom, common sense, or the intuitive mind. It is the place within us that *knows* how to live us. It does it every day in any number of ways. But it gets easily overlooked, due to the attention and disproportional significance attributed to our brain.

What so many of us have innocently misunderstood is that the brain is a machine to be used *in service* of our lives rather than like *the showrunner* to our lives. Misunderstanding its role can create a disempowered feeling whereby we feel obligated to believe whatever thoughts are experienced within the mind (particularly the sticky and persistent ones). We 'think' that because we experience 'insecurity' then such feelings reflect a fundamental truth about ourselves. Just because a feeling may be habitual, doesn't make it true. Such thoughts simply reflect what our machine brain is experiencing in that moment. Taking to heart thoughts as if they were the gospel is akin to feeling beholden to our alarm clock; the clock is merely telling us the time. It has no real power to *make* us get up. Similarly, our brain is merely telling us what thoughts we are experiencing in that moment. It has no real power to *make* us believe.

Have you ever noticed that true transformation and change never really come about through discipline or from the intellect, but rather from the intangible formless *knowing place* within all of us when we take the time to listen beyond our personal minds and thoughts? Wisdom is there guiding us. We've all experienced it throughout our lives, however fleeting. And when we do, it feels right. It feels like Truth. It feels like freedom. It feels like home.

Who we really are resides *beyond* thought and *before* thought, and in our clearest moments, radiates love, compassion, creativity, and common sense that is utterly devoid of insecurity. When we connect with who we really are, our personal minds tend to quiet down. When we are quiet and detached from personal thought, we see that everything else was a simple misunderstanding, and we can even be okay with criticism from others. We can feel uncomfortable without resorting to old patterns of behavior or thinking. We can distinguish *razzle-dazzle* noise from truth.

Criticism may be warranted and helpful to our own growth at times, but it can also be meaningless. Seeing personal thought for what it is allows the wisdom and common sense to rise up and guide us along the way.

In retrospect, I probably would have stayed at that party a little longer and sought out some people that were more welcoming and accepting (common sense rising up). I certainly would not have created a story about my worth in the eyes of those women, as I did. Manufacturing criticism of myself within my own mind no longer makes sense to me. I just didn't know that was what I was doing, all those years ago. At that time I was focused exclusively on the *content* of my thinking and trying to explain the *why* of it. What I didn't realize was that my experience was created *because* of the fact THAT I think. Period.

What This Lie Has Cost Me: I spent much of my time trying to be 'perfect' so as not to incur criticism. It was exhausting and ultimately futile since it assumed an element of control on my part. It also prevented me from speaking up and expressing my opinion when I felt the risk of criticism was too great. When I took the risk and was criticized, I agonized endlessly over what it meant about me personally and what I could do differently in the future.

What The Truth Tells Me: Control is an illusion. When I am connected to that place of love, compassion, wisdom, clarity, and confidence, I no longer see criticism as something personal, and as a result, I naturally know what to do or say or not do or say in the moment.

You don't need to put the yolk in the egg. The yolk is already in the egg.

-Valda Monroe

Reflection by Linda:

There's a quality that just sets some people apart. For me, that person was my high school classmate, Jackie. She was one of those girls who was smart, popular, and appeared to be overflowing with confidence.

To this day, I can see her in the classroom with her hand up, always eager to be called on by the teacher. She seemed fearless, never short of an opinion to share or a question to ask. There was a good reason why she always sat in the front row of the classroom, and I sat in the back; why she always played the leading role in school plays, while I opted to play minor roles that didn't utter a word. She would confidently and unabashedly speak her mind during those high school years, while I was embarrassed to hear the sound of my own voice. I so wanted to be like her.

I was in my early teens when I first started believing that girls like Jackie were born confident, and girls like me were born shy and insecure. In the same way that some of us are born tall, short, dark-skinned or blue-eyed, I used to think you either had the confidence gene or you didn't, and I believed I didn't.

Throughout my endeavor to rid myself of my insecurity, I would soon discover through the world of self-help that the feeling of confidence was actually something I could attain, but that it would take time and effort on my part. Later in life, the strategy I used to break out of my world of shyness and insecurity would have me reading hundreds of self-help books and attending countless workshops and seminars in which I would force myself to make a presentation in front of others in hopes of breaking the habit of being my shy self.

Some of those workshops were painfully challenging and embarrassing to me, but I was prepared to do whatever it took, no matter how awkward I felt. If they held the promise of transforming me on the inside into a confident *Jackie*-like young woman, I was up for all of it.

There is no doubt that those well-intentioned books and workshops helped me gain some understanding of why I suffered from insecurity. I learned that confidence was something we create, and that developing it was like strengthening or building a muscle. The more opportunities I had to exercise that muscle, the more I would experience confidence. The more I could practice acting as *if* I were confident and push through my fears, the more chance I would have of transforming myself from an awkward caterpillar into a beautiful butterfly.

I learned a lot about how to make my confidence muscle stronger, and it all seemed to make logical sense. But the task required a lot of diligence, hard work, and effort on my part to keep it going—to keep the positive-thinking plates spinning in the air. Every time I came back from a confidence-building workshop, I would feel as if I could take on the world, but then one week later, those same old insecure feelings would get all cozy with me again.

I invested a major part of life—almost thirty years—into not only believing that I was deficient and incomplete in this area, but also working hard to desperately change and fix the part of me that was lacking. So you can imagine how I felt when I heard a conversation that went like this:

Everyone is innately confident, and the only thing that makes some people feel a lack of confidence is their insecure thinking. You cannot NOT be confident.

This was both frustrating and exciting news—frustrating when I thought of all the time and money I had spent, and all the agony I had put myself through; but it was exciting to know that I've actually had confidence all along. It was as if someone had suddenly told me that I had an extra limb that I didn't know about and that I could have been using for all those years.

One of the false premises I (and everyone else) bought into while growing up was the idea that our feeling of confidence is a result of our accomplishments in life. Read any self-help book on how to gain confidence and you'll hear this over and over; that the more we accomplish, and the more we honor our accomplishments, the more we build the confidence muscle. It's as if all of our achievements should be listed on a "confidence resumé".

Jackie's "confidence resumé" read well: she was a great actor in school plays; she got good grades, and she had lots of friends. I believed her achievements produced her confidence.

When we think of confident people, we immediately equate them with their external success—their ability to make lots of money, look attractive, or speak effortlessly in front of hundreds of people.

But what I have come to discover is that confidence is not only innate, but completely independent of external circumstances and accomplishments. Even if we don't get to look great, even if we don't make a lot of money, even if we don't give eloquent speeches, even if we don't get to play the leading role in the school play, we can still feel confident, because true confidence is not about our *ability and what we achieve*—but is, rather, a certainty and deep knowing that we are whole and worthy no matter what we achieve. Babies and very young children are a great example of this. They've achieved nothing, they have no expertise in their young lives, they have no hair or teeth, and yet they exude confidence. In looking at them we realize that there is nothing to work on. And haven't we all come across people who are not physically attractive by conventional standards, or who don't have the gift of public speaking, but who nevertheless, exude confidence. Confidence does not have to be earned. There's nothing to fix, prove, make, create, alter or strive after.

In the same way our physical bodies have an immune system working to heal cuts and stop germs from making us sick, we also have a psychological immune system that keeps us mentally healthy. Both of these systems work brilliantly without any input on our part. The body and the mind are self-correcting. They know how to return us to a state of alignment and well-being without our intervention. That is, until we insert ourselves (our egos) in the middle of it all.

Like most people, I lived for years not knowing that my 'negative' thinking would go away all on its own, if I got out of the way. I was convinced

81

that I had to intervene just in case my situation got worse. Feeling 'negative' was a warning that something was wrong, that something had gone awry. Life isn't meant to be negative. Right? And if I allow myself to feel this way, I may run the risk of attracting more of it into my life. I kept hearing that 'like' attracts 'like'. The irony is that I lived a constant day to day struggle to be happy.

We find it difficult not to want to fix things, and we depend so much on the advice of others in the world of self-help who with all good intent, convince us that their "ten steps" will get us over our problems and allow us to feel good.

And so, instead of lightening our psychological load, we add more into the mix—more thinking, more analyzing, more probing. What we don't realize is that a mind that is filled with information and anxious thinking—a busy mind—causes the self-correcting system to jam up. We get our hands under the hood of the mind, so to speak, and start messing and tinkering around by holding onto thoughts that don't feel good, trying to over-think where we went wrong and why. And once you enter this swamp, it's very hard to get yourself out.

You'll know when the system has jammed-up because you will invariably feel stuck or uncomfortable in life. Whereas, if you've got nothing on your mind; if you don't get too cozy and intimate with your 'negative' thinking; if you allow the mind to clear itself—your innate qualities of clarity, self-assurance, and confidence will emerge effortlessly. Most of us don't know that the mind works this way, that it's designed for success.

There's a metaphor I love that explains how the mind is self-correcting. We've all at some time flooded our car carburetor with gasoline. We keep turning the engine over and over in an effort to start the car, but all it does is flood the carburetor. The solution? Stop for fifteen seconds and let the carburetor clear itself of gasoline—let it self-correct. When we do this, the car always starts effortlessly.

I'll never really know why Jackie seemed to have a natural proclivity towards confidence and I didn't. Maybe her parents encouraged and complimented her in her school work, unlike my parents, who rarely took an interest. Maybe her parents allowed her to express herself, whereas, my parents were always telling me to stop being so full of myself whenever I mentioned getting a gold star at school. But what I do know is that despite all of that, I do have clear memories when I'd feel completely at ease playing and dancing with my friends, never worrying about whether I was doing it in the right way, and I felt this way, regardless of whether my parents were supportive of me or not. I was just there in the moment, experiencing my confident self at play.

Was it true that Jackie showed up more confident than I was? Yes, it was true, but not because I missed out on the confidence gene. Maybe she just had a less-busy mind than I had at that time in our lives. And maybe that meant she didn't have as many feelings of unworthiness. When she felt insecure, maybe she didn't spend too much time thinking about it, whereas I would make a big deal out of it.

And if you're still thinking: *That's all well and good, but I still wish I had more confidence*, consider this piece of advice I heard from one of my colleagues, Mary Schiller who suggested we change our orientation from *self-help* to *self-discovery*. She gives the example of visiting a beautiful place like the Grand Canyon and posits that you would never think that the rim of the canyon needs to be moved, or the colors need to be darker, or the river re-routed. The idea of changing the Grand Canyon seems ludicrous. We go there to *discover* the beauty of the terrain not to improve it.

And it's no different with us. What if, instead, we avoided the self-help rhetoric of wanting to change and fix ourselves, and instead stepped into discovery mode? Because below all of our thoughts and the incessant thinking personal mind is everything that we already are...naturally. We know this on a bone-deep level—we've just gotten away from it with the emergence of our ego and all of our personal thinking.

Don't be afraid of finding out what and who you are and what is true of all experience. There's beauty in truth. To be confident is to be connected to your true nature. The Grand Canyon can't be less than it is, and neither can you.

What This Lie Has Cost Me: I spent decades feeling as if I was left out and not good enough—inferior to others because I didn't feel as confident as my friend. And that led me to decades of working on myself to fix something that was never broken or deficient in the first place.

What The Truth Tells Me: We are all innately confident. We all possess everything we need. None of us are left out.

*We are stars wrapped in skin – the light you are seeking has
always been within.*

-*Rumi*

Reflection by Lana:

Like all kids, I had wonder and curiosity about the world around me. I pondered where I had been before I was born and where I would go after I died. I puzzled over whether I had lived a life before this one, and whether angels and the tooth fairy truly existed.

In all of my speculation, however, I never truly appreciated the grace and beauty of the intelligent design and the wisdom that exists *within* nature and that *lives* nature each and every day.

I had never considered myself truly part of the natural world. Somehow I saw humans as separate. I thought we had our own special category given our immense cognitive advantages. In my innocent egocentric mind, I eschewed the fact that we were *part* of the natural world and as such we would be embraced by the same invisible laws of nature.

How different and humbling life looks when the invisible becomes visible and we begin to see that there is an intelligence that lives Life. It is what tilts the flower toward the sun, or the trees to shed their leaves, or the salmon to swim upstream. That intelligence is present in everything.

What is truly incredible, when viewed with humility and wonder, is how beautifully Life already knows *how* to live us. Seeing this play out in 'nature' reminds me of the wisdom and intelligence that resides within our own natural design...whether it be our physical immune system or our psychological immune system. Break an arm, it heals. Naturally. We may put a cast on the arm, but that cast is not the thing that is doing the healing. There is a deeper wisdom and intelligence at play that moves to fuse the bones back together.

The same goes for our psychological health and well-being. Feeling insecure? Wait a minute or two or ten. New thought and feeling will naturally come through to replace the insecure feeling. Emotions cannot be maintained indefinitely, despite our best efforts. It is part of our natural design.

More often than not, however, we forget or are simply unaware that such a deep intelligence exists within all of us. Instead, we rely on our intellect and personal mind to find resolutions to any problems we may face or uncomfortable feelings we may experience. As naturally born thinkers, we like to tinker within our minds...unaware that if left to do what it does naturally, our minds will settle and return us to balance and well-being. In other words, when we get out of our own way, Life has a way of providing an answer.

Growing up, I didn't recognize this. I thought I had to figure everything out on my own, using my intellect. I thought I had to think myself out of insecurity, and so I tended to double down on my intellectual efforts to find any kind of relief for uncomfortable insecure feelings. I read umpteen books, listened to umpteen audio tapes and attended umpteen trainings, all in an effort to find the 'right' remedy and the 'right' tool to distract me or relieve me from my feelings. It was all so much work and so much extra thinking. While some things I incorporated were well-meaning and wonderful in their own right, ultimately they were not sustainable and over time felt more like work than relief.

Believing that I needed to figure out a way to become confident or think my way to confidence or develop confidence merely added more stress and unnecessary thinking to my already 'insecure' mind. It was only when I realized for myself, that confidence was not something I had to force through 'correct' thinking or positive mantras...that confidence was a naturally occurring quality *beneath* all of my thinking, that I could finally take a breath and relax into who I really was. What reemerged more and more was that *true* me from the photo all those years ago that I thought was lost...or damaged.

My relief came in finally understanding that there was nothing *to do* to create confidence and that the Intelligence that governed all of Life, also had my back. When I got out of the way with my personal thinking about whether or not I was confident and how it should look if I was, confidence naturally emerged. These days I know, more often than not, that by showing up to life with an open and curious mind, I can trust that, as part of the Natural world, I am also bequeathed with all of the common sense, wisdom, clarity and *confidence* needed from moment to moment.

And when I forget, I know that I am in a temporary thought storm that will pass.

There is a beauty and an elegance and an intelligence running the show, that, when truly seen can humbly bring us to our knees and relieve us of our unnecessary, but well-meaning, efforts to achieve the same through our intellect.

This innate intelligence that is living the world is a gift to us all. Freely given.

If I have lost confidence in myself I have the Universe against me.

-*Ralph Waldo Emerson*

Reflection by Linda:

When I first started dating my husband, I went through an uncomfortable phase of not really knowing whether he loved me as much as I loved him. I wanted so much to relax in my love for him—to give-in and let my affections be known. But I purposefully put the brakes on and held myself back out of fear and insecurity that he may not care for me in the same way.

I've come to see that the act of falling in love is a perfect metaphor for the relationship we each have with that larger than life partner—the Universe. The dynamics are exactly the same. And wouldn't you know, there are just as many variations of how that relationship gets played out.

Some of us show up with high expectations knowing that the Universe has the potential to be one great partner—a partner that is always working with us and has our best interest. We dive right into this relationship. We're optimistic, unabashed, playful, trusting, and eager to do whatever it takes to keep our relationship vibrant. We take the risk because we know that the price of missing out on getting plugged into the enormous power that the Universe has to offer, would be too great of a loss.

And then there are some of us who can never quite relax, let go, and trust that the Universe really loves us and has our back—we don't really know for sure that it wants to power us and support us through life. We believe we have to take full control of our future. We believe we're in this life all on our own with our own capabilities and intellect. And so we hold the relationship at arm's length…just in case something goes wrong…just in case it's not as benevolent and honorable as we had hoped.

Albert Einstein said that there is only one question worth asking; the answer to which determines your entire outlook on life and affects everything that you desire for yourself.

Do you believe the Universe is friendly or unfriendly?

I've personally spent too many years fearing the Universe and trying to go at this life alone. And why wouldn't I? The Universe is BIG and POWERFUL. And I'm so tiny in comparison. Why would the Universe have any interest in little me?

The fact that we may doubt that the Universe is friendly is our first big misunderstanding. Take a moment to acknowledge that there is so much going on behind the scenes in life without our conscious awareness, and without us having to do anything. We have a sun and a moon relentlessly and consistently doing their job; we have lungs that breathe us; and we have gravity to keep us from falling down. The cut on my hand heals all on its own; and the planets are spinning around as I write this chapter.

It's hard not to see that there is a life force and intelligence that is connecting and energizing everything from the tiny blade of grass to the vast ocean. All is included, and everything is powered by an invisible force. That same force is also powering us. Why wouldn't it? Why would we be left out?

Author and coach, Michael Neill describes how he once observed a mom pushing a supermarket cart fashioned to look like a car with her young boy sitting in the seat, hands on the make-shift steering wheel turning it left and right, as if he was controlling the direction they were going. Of course, we know that it was actually his mother doing all of the steering. The young child didn't know that fact yet because of his age. But there would come a day when that "game" wouldn't make much sense to him anymore, because he would understand that there's really someone else, some other power (his mom) that's helping him steer the cart.

The idea that there is an energy and intelligence behind everything in life is a universal belief. Most religions and philosophies—even within the science of quantum physics—believe that every form of life is being powered by a universal force. There's a lot going on without us having to do anything. A huge weight is lifted from us just knowing that we're not in this life all alone.

True confidence is allowing ourselves to get plugged into that source of universal power—to be fully in that supportive and connected relationship, in the same way that I finally surrendered to professing my love for my husband. When we see the interplay between our own personal minds and the role of Universal mind—when we operate in harmony by driving our carts together through life—that's when life becomes beautiful and bountiful—that's when we thrive.

We've all had the experience of being confused and bewildered when an electrical device fails to work—thinking that there's something more serious going on with the mechanics—only to discover that it simply wasn't plugged into the electrical source. And it's the same with our own lives. How often have we gotten caught up with trying to troubleshoot our problems with our intellect alone? When we switch off or drop our personal thinking, we actually invite a deeper wisdom and creativity to flow through us. It is ours for the taking.

There's no guarantee that a love relationship with someone else is going to take hold or last forever. My husband could have failed to reciprocate my love for him, and he may even lose his love for me in the future. But the relationship we all have with the Universe is and always has been a given, a constant, and is guaranteed to show up and support us in the same way that gravity and the changing of the seasons never let us down.

When my husband and I finally acknowledged our love and trust for each other, our relationship naturally became deeper and more satisfying. We were able to exhale, finally relax, and create a beautiful life together. And it's no different with the Universe—with the invisible energy that connects it all together. That vast formless intelligence that is powering and supporting everything, wants to experience itself in form. We are a living, breathing creative process in a dance with the Universe. And through this process we get to play, write, build, cook, paint, love, and live our lives to the fullest knowing that there is an intelligence that is supporting us along the way. It's for sure a friendly Universe—one where there's only love.

Life is either a daring adventure, or nothing.

–Helen Keller

By now you have probably recognized yourself in the stories we've shared about our own struggles with confidence and the lies we tell ourselves. Our shared experience points to a very important truth: *We are all in the same boat.* Not only do we all experience feelings of insecurity and un-worthiness from time to time, but we all face the same challenge: ***How to know the true source of our feelings and what is true of all humans.***

Our suffering arises when we mistakenly believe that our thoughts and feelings are telling us something fundamentally true about who we are as a person. We innocently compound our pain with more insecure thinking and story-building within our minds. Our confusion and suf-fering begins the moment we believe that the source of our feeling is something OTHER than *thought in the moment.*

Simply put, insecurity is a temporary feeling that has nothing to do with who we really are. *We know this* when we look deeper in our quiet moments. We know that wisdom, common sense, resiliency and confidence have been present and available to us throughout the whole of our lives.

It is easy to get caught up in our thinking, especially when we are experiencing an uncomfortable feeling such as insecurity. We want to get rid of it as quickly as possible. Naturally, we look to our intellect for the answer. As charmingly illustrated in the book, *Winnie-the-Pooh*, the brain rarely provides the understanding we need, however:

"Rabbit's clever," said Pooh thoughtfully.

"Yes," said Piglet, "Rabbit's clever."

"And he has a brain."

"Yes," said Piglet. "Rabbit has a brain."

There was a long silence.

"I suppose," said Pooh,— "that's why he never understands anything…"

As we have indicated throughout this book, having insecure thoughts is normal. They will come and go, as will every feeling we experience. There is nothing to be done. The understanding we have shared is not a *prescription* to be applied, but rather a *description* of how things work. When we get out of the way, the system works brilliantly and will naturally return us to common sense and well-being. When we mistakenly get in the way of the system, by innocently adding unnecessary thought, we temporarily jam it and move ourselves further away from our natural and optimal innate health.

In the book, *I am that*, Nisargadatta Maharaj states,

The disease is simple and the remedy is equally simple. It is your mind only that makes you insecure and unhappy. Anticipation makes you insecure, memory – unhappy. Stop misusing your mind and all will be well with you. You need not set it right – it will set itself right. It will set itself right as soon as you give up all concern with the past and the future and live entirely in the now.

Funnily enough, even while writing this book, I experienced a bout of insecure thought. In fact, I pretty much experienced every lie we've outlined in the book within the space of a few days. At the time it felt so real. Once again, I was sure there was something wrong with me. I was so caught up in my thinking that I couldn't see the truth. What eventually clued me into the way I was innocently misunderstanding my experience was the uncomfortable, fractured feeling of insecurity. Once I caught onto that, I realized that my feelings were simply indicating where my thinking was in the moment. The busier my mind became as it tried to dig into the content of my experience, the more insecure I felt.

What I recognized and continue to recognize is that my feelings of insecurity are just a reflection of thought in the moment and that there is no need to *create* a story or *blame* a circumstance or *manage* a mind. When I wake up to this truth and once again see that we are naturally designed to return home to that place of wisdom and clarity and confidence, I relax into a space that allows me to show up fully and gratefully to Life.

It is in these moments that I realize, we are never really *insecure*, we only *think* we are.

Much love,
Lana

*It takes tremendous courage to admit to yourself that
you are not defective in any way whatsoever.*

–*Cheri Huber*

Throughout this book we've described the most common lies we tell ourselves about our insecurities—about why we think we're not confident. I used to hold on tight to my lies—my misunderstandings—because I believed that they would keep me safe, secure, and protected. But the truth is, those lies robbed me of my potential and uniqueness. And the tragedy is that I missed out on opportunities when it came to creating the life I really wanted to live and who I wanted to BE in that life. I missed out on experiencing the exhilarating freedom of being my true self.

Can you see how the lies you tell yourself keep you from being your true self?

Throughout our stories we have tried to convey **three Universal truths**:

1. At our core, we are innately full of well-being and confidence—we are not broken, and there is nothing about us that we have to fix.

2. The mind is self-correcting and is designed for success.

3. The mind only works one way—from the inside-out.

When we understand these truths, we'll not only get some insight into how we have been getting in our own way, but we'll also discover that life becomes so much simpler. Our fears, anxieties, and insecurities will not be a mystery or obstacle to us anymore. We will understand where our experience of insecurity is coming from.

Whatever lie you've been telling yourself is just your innocent attempt at trying to find comfort and relief from life's fears and anxieties. Sydney Banks writes: "Everyone in this world shares the same innate source of wisdom, but it is hidden by the tangle of our own misguided personal thoughts." Feeling insecure just means that you're giving your insecure thoughts more power than they deserve.

You may be wondering after reading this book, why you still feel insecure, or why you don't suddenly feel confident. You may have grasped a new understanding of how the mind works, but wonder at what point will I see my insecurities melt away? The truth is: There will never come a time when you'll be totally free of experiencing insecure thinking. You will still have moments when you shy away from speaking up at meetings, prefer to stay in the background, act overly deferential when a man is in your presence; believe that you have to have a relationship (or something else) to make your life complete; and you'll still continue to invite that crazy voice in your head to run the show and convince you all over again, that you're not good enough.

In the world of self-help there's a very well-meaning drive to get us to believe that we need to be worked on and improved—that if we could just shed our insecurities and any other 'negative' feeling, we would finally live up to our potential and finally feel wonderful. It's a nice idea, but it doesn't reflect the reality of where our experience comes from. We're going to continually feel the wonderful mix of joy and despair, happiness and unhappiness, insecurity and confidence. That's the human experience. But the difference now is that you know the source of your experience. You know that every bit of negative "weather" you get to live through is normal and transitory. And that's going to make all the difference in your life.

My insecure feelings still pop up like a cork on the water. But the difference now is that I know that it's just thought in the moment creating a feeling. And I know that when those thoughts inevitably float by, like the clouds in the sky, the true confidence that is me—that blue sky—will shine through again and reveal itself, because the blue sky is always there under the clouds. There is tremendous freedom knowing how the equipment of the mind works.

I'd like to leave you with one last personal story:

I was only nineteen when I left London with my boyfriend to travel overland en route to Australia. Our journey took four long months of hitching rides with some very dubious characters along the way, and endless travel on buses, trains, boats, and planes.

It was a great adventure—albeit arduous and dangerous—for someone so young and inexperienced. I don't know how I had the confidence and courage to do it, because there were moments when I nearly lost my life.

For example, when a Turkish truck driver pulled a knife on my boyfriend because he wanted to kidnap me, and I poured my coffee over him, so that we could run away. Or the treacherous bus ride we took through the Khyber Pass in the mountains of Afghanistan, knowing all too well there was a threat of being attacked by armed bandits. And the most unnerving of all—being the only woman traveling for ten days on a hippie bus with thirty young sex-starved men.

I have lots of stories that reveal my confidence. They are stories that make me both shudder and marvel at how my tender young self ever survived them. I won't deny that there was some naiveté on my part, but I also know that despite my insecurities and fears, my experiences were proof that my confidence and wisdom was there within me all along.

And yet, later on in my life…

When it came to believing I was smart enough to go to college (I enrolled for college at the age of 35); confident enough to know I could be perfectly happy living without a man; confident enough to speak up and hear the sound of my own voice; confident enough to believe I had a point of view or a preference; confident enough to apply for a job that would challenge me; or confident enough to ask for a higher salary...

My confidence was seemingly nowhere to be found.

I wish I wasn't so insecure is a common refrain I hear from women. They want the confidence to do so many things in their lives, and experience true freedom. But they just don't believe they have it in them.

The truth is: We all have it in us. No-one is exempt. We've always had it. But don't take my word for it.

Consider everything you've done in your life and how you've somehow or other put your insecurities aside and channelled your confidence—not just in big and bold experiences (like travelling the world), but in the everyday ordinary events of your life.

Let's remind ourselves that despite all of our fears, inhibitions, insecurities, and doubts:

We had the confidence to walk, fall down and get up again.

We had the confidence to go to school for the first time.

We had the confidence to paint our first picture and show it to others.

We had the confidence to audition for the choir and let someone hear our voice.

We had the confidence to fall in love and risk having our heart broken.

We had the confidence to really look someone in the eye.

We had the confidence to not be afraid of feeling sadness.

We had the confidence to say *I love you, or I don't love you anymore.*

We had the confidence to admit that our work deadened our spirit.

We had the confidence to move away from a life we didn't want.

We had the confidence to question the direction of our life.

We had the confidence to expect more for our lives.

We had the confidence to stand up for someone else.

We had the confidence to change the trajectory of our lives.

Sit with this list. Look at your life for your own evidence. Take it all in. Savor it. These are truly the BIG confident moments. Recognize that you've had confidence all along, even when you didn't think so. Acknowledge where it has shown up in your life. Realize that your confidence is as intact as your fingerprints.

We cannot NOT be confident.

If I could go back and speak to my nineteen-year-old self, here's what I would now say to her:

Sweetheart, you don't have to worry so much about being liked by others. Don't be afraid of being alone. Look inside yourself more often. Listen to that quiet inner voice and honor it. Don't believe everything you think. Accept yourself as you are—there's nothing wrong with you. Be true to yourself—don't compromise your integrity. Don't let your feelings of insecurity stop you from going after what you really want. Don't play small. Value your own opinions. Know that your happiness and peace are not dependent on other people or outside circumstances, but are self-generated. Be gentle and kind with yourself. Place more emphasis on being respected than being liked. Take time to get out of your head, and don't over-think things. Take action, take risk, don't be afraid to fail, and stop apologizing for who you are. Know that you are more powerful than you realize. These are not lies. This is the TRUTH.

The Buddha once said:

"Just as we can know the ocean because it always tastes of salt, we can recognize enlightenment (the truth) because it always tastes of freedom."

Not comfort. Not ease. Freedom.

Here's to your confident life.

Much love,

Linda

ACKNOWLEDGEMENTS

A special thanks to Sydney Banks who is behind the understanding outlined in this book. To our mentors—Robin Charbit and Sandy Krot, who were generous with their time and deep insights into the content of this book. To Ali Duffy for her meticulous editing skills. To Olivia Dickson for the design and layout of the book cover. To our readers, Sue Cross, Rose Dalton, Kate Lundberg, and Gayle Noble. And last, but not least to our family members, especially our wonderful husbands, Peter and Tim who have been there with us through all of our insecurities and doubts, and who never stopped encouraging us to keep going.

Lana Bastianutti

As a lifelong learner and explorer of life, Lana believes that any transformation begins on the inside. As a coach, she has the uncanny ability to dig deep and help her clients uncover life-changing realizations…as well as finding and appreciating the humor in almost any situation.

Lana is the mother of two young women and wife of 26 years (and counting!) She holds a degree in Psychology and a Master's degree in Industrial Relations. She obtained her coaching certification from Concordia University and the Brooke Castillo Life Coach School. Lana gained additional coaching accreditation from The Robbins-Madanes Center founded by personal development expert Tony Robbins and world-renowned psychotherapist, Cloe Madanes.

More recently Lana's coaching and life have been transformed by the work of Sydney Banks. She has personally attended training sessions and retreats with Dr. George Pransky, Dr. Amy Johnson, Dr. Dicken Bettinger, Dr. Ken Manning, Robin Charbit, Sandy Krot, Byron Katie and Steve Chandler. Lana writes a weekly blog that informs, entertains and challenges her readers and has ventured into podcasting. Lana resides in Lexington, Massachusetts with her husband and can be found online at LanaBcoaching.com.

Linda Ford

Linda is a certified master coach and teacher at heart. She has always been deeply curious about the nature of transformation and the human potential, which has led her to spend decades steeped in the world of self-help, both as a practitioner and a coach. She has been personally trained by Dr. Martha Beck, *New York Times* bestselling author.

Linda holds a Master's degree in English Literature. Her professional background includes teaching English and working in the world of international development. She has personally attended training sessions with Dr. Dicken Bettinger, Dr. Ken Manning, and Robin Charbit.

Linda currently lives with her husband, Tim and dog Scout in Rockport, Massachusetts. For more information please visit: Lindafordcoaching.com

This edition of

Women and Confidence:
The Truth about The Lies We Tell Ourselves

is designed by Will Mancini. The typefaces used in the interior are Caslon, Palatino Linotype, and Wonderfall. The typefaces used on the cover are Zeitung Pro, Brandon Grotesque, and Wonderfall.

More designs can be found at wmancini.com

Printed in Great Britain
by Amazon